MAKING THE RIGHT CONNECTIONS

MAKING THE RIGHT CONNECTIONS
Michael Larkin

Copyright © Michael Larkin.
All rights reserved.

Published by Book Hub Publishing.

First Edition 2019

No part of this publication, including the cover,
may be reproduced, reprinted, or transmitted by any method,
or utilised in any format, including photocopying, recording,
information storage systems, or any other means,
without the prior written permission of the author.

Much of the information and content of this book has been handed down over several generations.
Time may have altered some facts, statements, quotes, etc.
Any misspellings, omissions or errors are regretted.
The author, booksellers, graphic designer, printers and others associated with its publication
will not be liable for any improper or incorrect references, photographic credits, misquotes,
or other unintentional omissions and no responsibility whatsoever
is accepted for any loss, inconvenience or damage arising from errors,
inaccuracies or interpretations which may be expressed here.

Cover and Book Design and Layout:
Declan Durcan, Cloontubrid, Ross, Castlebar, County Mayo.
086 2658038 decdurcan@gmail.com

Proofread by Karen Gallen.

ISBN: 978-1-9164848-1-8

All imagery and photographs strictly copyright as indicated in captions or with the author.

www.bookhubpublishing.com
091/846953 087/2246885 Twitter: @bookhubpublish Instagram: bookhub_publishing

For further information re international distribution contact info@bookhubpublishing.com

Michael Larkin may be booked to speak or present on the themes of the book by contacting niall@bookhubpublishing.com

DEDICATION

This book is dedicated to the countless thousands of Irish emigrants
who departed from an island ravaged by famine and despair,
in the hope of securing a better way of life in foreign lands,
with the eternal dream of someday returning to the land of their birth.

It is also dedicated to those, who, for whatever reason,
lost that vital connection to their families, friends or homeland.

ABOUT THE AUTHOR

"Don't allow the mists of time erase the spoken words of our ancestors"

Michael Larkin is a firm believer in 'writing down' and recording the spoken words from yesterday, so that future generations will appreciate the lives and journeys of our ancestors.

Throughout his professional career in the field of mental health with the Health Service Executive, he constantly highlighted the benefits of creative writing as part of a holistic approach towards positive mental health and wellbeing.

A recipient of a 'Mayo People of the Year Award' 2017, as Chairman of the editorial team of the highly acclaimed book, 'Ballyheane Past & Present', he has also written for a number of magazines, journals and Irish networks abroad, including the Irish American Cultural Institute, American Conference for Irish Studies, Ireland-US Council, etc.

An advocate of fostering and promoting closer links with the County Mayo and Irish diaspora overseas, he has attended a number of Mayo World Conventions and other diaspora related networking events.

He interacts regularly with members of the Mayo.ie team, is a contributor to the Destination Mayo Tourism Strategy and collaborates regularly with a number of tour operators in co-ordinating itineraries for incoming visitors to County Mayo.

A founding member and first chairman of his local community council, he is a member of various knowledge transfer and information sharing groups, a former member of Junior Chamber Ireland and is actively involved in fundraising and supporting many charitable and voluntary organisations.

ACKNOWLEDGEMENTS

At the outset, may I express in the most genuine way possible, a sincere 'Thank You', to a number of very special individuals and friends, some, unfortunately no longer with us, who have contributed to the compilation of this book.

In keeping with the theme of the book's title, many interesting and special connections have emerged - some new, many reawakened from their dormant past.

On what has been, and continues to be, an amazing journey of discovery, I wish to sincerely thank Mr. James Lamb, Honorary Irish Consul and President of the Irish Institute of Pittsburgh, for co-ordinating a series of meetings, assisting with research and ensuring that my journey to Pittsburgh was both enjoyable and productive. To Mr. Edward Galloway, Archives & Special Collections Director, University of Pittsburgh, thank you for your guidance and assistance.

Similarly, Mr. Peter Gilmore, Adjunct Prof. of History, Carlow University, Prof. Andrew E. Masich, President & C.E.O. Senator John Heinz History Center, and the representatives from many of the Irish cultural networks, historical societies, educational institutions, etc. thank you all for your input.

Meeting with Ms. Gerry McLaughlin, President of the Fort Pitt Pioneer Chapter, Pittsburgh, and other members from this chapter was extremely special. The significance of this connection was marked in 2016 when Ms. McLaughlin, together with her husband John made that special journey to County Mayo and laid a bell shaped wreath at the headstone of Thomas Larkin.

Prof. Timothy McMahon, President of the American Conference for Irish Studies (A.C.I.S.), Dr. Matthew O'Brien, Prof. of History, thank you both for adopting this story as a true symbol of Irish American connectivity.

The degree of knowledge and expertise of Mr. William Caughlin, Corporate Archivist AT&T, is unrivalled in relation to the history of the early days of the telephone industry in N. America. Thank you for enriching me with your knowledge. Grateful thanks to the Executive Director of the Telephone Pioneers, Ms. Charlene Hill, and Ms. Shirley Zunich, for welcoming me so warmly to their headquarters in Denver.

To Mr Roddy Feely, Executive Director of the Ireland - U.S. Council, thank you for inviting me to display some of Thomas Larkin's memorabilia at one of your prestigious events.

Special acknowledgement also to Mr. Greg Varisco, Chief Operations Officer, Aqua Comms, for vividly illustrating the connection between Thomas Larkin's time as a Telephone Pioneer in America, and the role of today's Pioneers, or innovators, in the provision of ultra modern worldwide connectivity.

In selecting the theme 'Mayo - the Connected County', for the Mayo World Convention 2014, the organising committee kindly accepted Thomas Larkin's journey and the arrival of a new, highly sophisticated transatlantic fiber optic cable, as an excellent symbol of connectivity - past, present and future - Thank You.

Without the expertise and professionalism of Mr Declan Durcan, Graphic Designer, this book would still be in its infancy. In addition, Mr Durcan enthusiastically embraced the story and had the vision to ensure the entire concept became the publication you now hold. I wish to greatly acknowledge your energy and commitment from start to finish.

A sincere thanks to Ms. Caitriona Doyle for your words of encouragement and the countless hours spent transcribing much handwritten material.

A special acknowledgement also to the many Mayo Associations Worldwide, diaspora networks and other alliances, who have lent support.

To Micheál and Shane Larkin, thank you both for your unwavering support and being part of this amazing journey.

Wonderful friends Mary and Tom Treacy, together with Fr. Michael Treacy, have unflinchingly supported this publication, from the beginning. Thank you all.

Grateful thanks to a small number of special friends who took the time to read early drafts of this book. To Mayo County Council / Mayo.ie, especially Martina Hughes, Head of Communications and Neil Sheridan, Communications and Diaspora AO, your support is appreciated.

John Healy, Country View Columnist, Mayo News and Tony Deffely, former Head of Castlebar College of Further Education, thank you both for your advice and feedback. To Niall and the team at Book Hub Publishing, for your eagle-eyed editing, guidance and support, thank you.

To Mr Austin Vaughan, County Librarian, Mr. Ivor Hamrock, Ms. Maureen Costello, your assistance is greatly appreciated. Grateful appreciation and acknowledgement also to the many individuals and sources for photographs included throughout the book. Their inclusion greatly enhances and provides a greater understanding of the context that the book is intended to portray from an educational and visual perspective. While it would be invidious to acknowledge all sources individually, please accept a sincere and general 'Thank You'.

Also acknowledged in advance, is the support of all of you who may purchase this book, either for yourselves, friends or members of our diaspora throughout the world.

To anyone who feels their contribution has not been acknowledged, my sincere apologies.

Once again, to anyone who contributed in any way,
a most sincere 'Thank You'.

"This book provides a valuable contribution to the communication story. It is also a valuable contribution to the story of Irish emigration and the building of a modern America. Not least it's a sharing of the historic contribution of a member of the Larkin family in the past and the part he played in the foundation of the global communication systems that we have today".
Enda Kenny TD, former Taoiseach (Prime Minister) 2011-2017.

"Richly illustrated, this lively account of Irish American connectivity touches upon a number of the strands that make up the strong relationship between Ireland and the USA today. Thomas Larkin's pioneering journey, the invention and evolution of the telephone, transatlantic fiber optic cables, all of those themes are merged together as symbols of today's varied transatlantic connections.
Dr. Matthew O'Brien PhD, Pittsburgh, Professor of History, Author and member of the American Conference for Irish Studies.

"This interesting and wide-ranging book traces the career of a Mayo-born emigrant to the U.S.A. and the return to his native land, as well as many of the technological innovations in global communications that he experienced on both sides of the Atlantic".
Bernard O'Hara, Author, Historian and former lecturer NUI Galway.

"A must read book for Irish Americans and Irish born. Making the Right Connections takes us on a journey from the tranquil, rural townland of Derrew in County Mayo to the mile high city of Denver, Colorado, from Ballyheane to Boston, Castlebar to Cleveland, and Mayo to Manhattan, all separated by the Atlantic ocean, yet uniquely connected through Thomas Larkin's career pathway".
Gerry Quinn, President, Mayo Society of Greater Cleveland.

"Here is a terrific story about a young man from a rural village in Ireland, who, like so many of his friends, emigrated to the U.S.A., simply to find employment. As a distinguished member of the Bell Telephone Company in Pennsylvania, he made a significant contribution to the telephone industry in the early 1900s".
Terry Reilly, Author, Historian and former Editor of the Western People.

CONTENTS

◈ FOREWORD ◈

◈ ABOUT THIS BOOK ◈

◈ INTRODUCTION ◈

◈ CHAPTERS ◈

Ch 1. Before the Journey ~ *Page 7*

Ch 2. The Journey Begins ~ *Page 17*

Ch 3. The Development of the Telephone ~ *Page 25*

Ch 4. Thomas Larkin, From Philadelphia to Pittsburgh ~ *Page 35*

Ch 5. Mayos' World Champions of the Time ~ *Page 49*

Ch 6. The Telephone Pioneers of America ~ *Page 55*

Ch 7. The Homecoming ~ *Page 59*

Ch 8. My Journey ~ *Page 71*

Ch 9. Thomas Larkin's Legacy - A Symbol of Transatlantic Connectivity ~ *Page 87*

Ch 10. A Unique Tapestry of Connectivity ~ *Page 91*

Ch 11. Reflection ~ *Page 93*

◈ AN ODE TO TELEPHONE PIONEERS OF YESTERYEAR ◈

FOREWORD

As President of the Fort Pitt Telephone Pioneer Chapter, Pittsburgh, Pennsylvania, United States of America, it was my privilege and pleasure to have become acquainted with the author of this book, Michael Larkin, in February 2015. What began with a letter from Michael, followed by a series of back and forth telephone conversations and e-mails, has evolved into a true pioneering friendship. In a similar way to Irish Americans visiting Ireland to discover their Irish roots and heritage, Michael was determined to unearth a little more information and perhaps 'walk' in at least some of the footsteps of his Telephone Pioneer of America ancestor Thomas Larkin.

Visiting Pittsburgh in 2016, and again in 2018, he participated in one of our community projects, addressed one of our luncheons, and together we explored the streets on the south side of Pittsburgh, where Thomas Larkin once resided.

In what was a further rekindling of this almost forgotten connection, in October 2016, representing the New Vision Pioneers of the United States of America, we undertook a very poignant and special visit to County Mayo, where, together with members of the Larkin family and friends, at the final resting place of Thomas Larkin, we placed three white carnations, signifying fellowship, loyalty and service, which together form our Pioneer triangle, the foundation of our organisation.

This book gives us an overview of Thomas Larkin's emigrant journey to the U.S.A. But, in many ways it is every emigrant's story. It also encompasses other themes which symbolise the many special connections that exist between Ireland and the U.S.A.

The 'American Wake', held before a son, daughter, or other family member departed for the U.S.A, the 'American Dream' of an immigrant arriving in the New World, are contrasting reminders and images of Irish migration in the past.

The initial scepticism and doubt regarding the prospect of the telephone ever becoming a commercial success, significant milestones in the evolution of telecommunications, transatlantic fiber optic cables, handwritten letters with 'news' from America, connections made and lost through waves of emigration, all of those topics are vividly portrayed within this book.

Making the Right Connections reminds us of a time when twitter referred to the chirping sound of birds in the trees, spam referred to tinned ham, rather than an unsolicited message, and the input of a telephone operator was required to transact a telephone call.

The early Telephone Pioneers transformed communications around the world. Thomas Larkin, throughout his distinguished career with the Bell Telephone Company in Pennsylvania, helped to create many of the connections required to ensure the success of this transformation.

Today, the Pioneers continue the proud legacy of the original Telephone Pioneers by 'answering the call of those in need' through a variety of educational, environmental and life enrichment community projects.

Making the Right Connections will ensure that this precious link to the past and the legacy of Thomas Larkin, Telephone Pioneer of America, will be preserved for future generations.

Gerry McLaughlin,
President of the Fort Pitt Telephone Pioneer Chapter,
Pittsburgh, Pennsylvania, United States of America.

ABOUT THIS BOOK

This book reminds us of a time when the handwritten letter, a telegram or wire, operator assisted telephone calls and radio, were the means by which news of worldwide events and happenings were transmitted. In today's world of instantaneous connectivity, its interesting to note that it was as 'recent' as 1983, when cellular or mobile phones became commercially available for the first time. The first delivery of mail 'by air' between North America and Ireland occurred on June 15th 1919, when John Alcock and Arthur W. Brown made the first non-stop flight across the Atlantic Ocean. Following the invention of the telephone by A.G. Bell in 1876, many observers deemed his device to be little more than a 'gadget', which would never achieve commercial success.

Thomas Larkin, born in County Mayo on July 4th 1874, similar to thousands of Irishmen and women, crossed the Atlantic Ocean to the 'New World' in search of work. His 'American Dream' became a reality when he secured employment with the Bell Telephone Company of Pennsylvania, and as one of the early Telephone Pioneers of America, he helped to deliver what was then, new methods of communication over wires. Who was Thomas Larkin? Who were the Telephone Pioneers of America? Why, in 2016, did the President of the Fort Pitt Telephone Pioneer Chapter, Pittsburgh, make a special visit to County Mayo to lay a bell shaped wreath at the headstone of this man? Why did the President and members of the American Conference for Irish Studies (ACIS) deem it fitting to acknowledge the legacy of this Telephone Pioneer of America?

This book provides a fascinating insight, not only into the journey of one Irish emigrant and the history of the telephone, it also encompasses much of the social history of Ireland and the United States in the early 1900s.

The 'connections' made by A. G. Bell, Samuel Morse, Thomas Larkin, and other great pioneers from the past, have paved the way for today's 'web' of worldwide connectivity.

INTRODUCTION

"TRAVEL THE WORLD WHILE YOU CAN, GO WHERE YOU WANT TO GO,
HOW I WISH I HAD MADE THAT JOURNEY WHEN I WAS A YOUNGER MAN".

I vividly recall the above words, spoken by John Koster, who I met for the first time at his home in New Jersey a number of years ago. Mr Koster, at the time in his eighties, was a grandson of Margaret Larkin (sister of Thomas Larkin), who had emigrated from County Mayo in 1886. How he lamented never having set foot, or 'walked' on the ground of his ancestors here in County Mayo - now it was too late. With a quiver in his voice and tears in his eyes, he gazed at the photographs of the old homestead and deeply regretted never having touched the stones of its crumbling walls.

Were his words conveying a message that I should pay attention to?

Research carried out by the National University of Ireland (N.U.I.), Maynooth, reveal that the townland of Killawalla, County Mayo, suffered the largest population decline in Ireland during the famine era. Between 1841- 1851, the region lost two thirds of its population. Surrounding townlands throughout County Mayo and most of the western seaboard also witnessed similar reductions in population. Thousands of young men and women emigrated to Great Britain, thousands more undertook that perilous voyage across the Atlantic Ocean in search of a better future in the 'New World'.

In today's highly connected world, it's difficult to envisage the length of time it took for messages or news from sons and daughters who had emigrated to reach their homeland. When we consider that the RMS Titanic, on its maiden voyage, collected over 1,200 sacks of mail in Queenstown, it gives us an indication of the amount of written correspondence being transported in both directions across the Atlantic at the time. It was as 'recent' as January 7th, 1927 before the first official transatlantic telephone call was successfully made between New York and London. For many years following its invention by Alexander G. Bell in 1876, the telephone was deemed to be a luxury and an unnecessary item of expenditure.

INTRODUCTION

"That's an amazing invention Mr Bell, but who would ever want to use it?" was President Rutherford B. Hayes' response to Bell, on his viewing of the telephone for the first time.

Radio, T.V., internet, mobile or cellular phones, e-mail, Skype, etc. and many other forms of advanced communication have revolutionised our methods of connectivity today.

The recent completion of the transatlantic fiber optic cable, linking Shirley, New York to Killala, County Mayo and the planned installation of a second fiber optic cable, between New Jersey and Westport, County Mayo, ensures that the title 'the Connected County' belongs to Mayo.

Thomas Larkin was just one other Irish emigrant, who made that transatlantic voyage, arriving at the port of Philadelphia on May 25th, 1899. Similar to thousands of other Irish exiles, his mission was simple - to seek employment in the New World and hopefully some day to return to his native homeland. In keeping with the theme of this book, securing employment with the Bell Telephone Company of Pennsylvania ensured that the word 'connectivity' would become a key word in Thomas Larkin's long and distinguished career with that company.

In the old Larkin homestead in Derrew, similar to most Irish homes of this era, on the mantlepiece over the open fireplace and on the walls, small black and white photographs of family members long since deceased, signified a link to times past, or to those who had emigrated. Alongside, were much larger 18"×12" (46cm x 30cm) pictures of the Sacred Heart, with a permanently lit red lamp beneath, a picture of Pope John XXIII and a similar size picture of President John F. Kennedy, signifying the strong Catholic faith and connectivity to the United States of America.

However, of even greater significance, in the context of this book, were some rare and special memorabilia relating to Thomas Larkin's career as a Telephone Pioneer of America.

Those tarnished and worn items, coupled with the words spoken by John Koster at the commencement of this introduction, triggered my resolve to someday discover a little more about Thomas Larkin, his journey, connections made and lost, predictions regarding the telephone and the advances in communication through the generations.

Similar to the transatlantic fiber optic cable connecting the United States of America with County Mayo, this book aims to take you on a unique journey of connectivity, from a time of the handwritten letter, telegraph, operator assisted telephone, right up to the present day.

I hope you find it enjoyable, informative and perhaps even a little bit inspirational.

*"Believe me, the day will come
when you will be able to see the person
who you are speaking to on the telephone"*

(Thomas Larkin, born July 4th, 1874)

*"I believe that in the not too distant future,
it will be possible to have dinner in New York
at seven o clock in the evening
and breakfast in Dublin or London the following morning"*

(Alexander G. Bell, born March 3rd, 1847)

Pastoral scene in the townland of Derrew. *Pic.: Michael Larkin.*

1

BEFORE THE JOURNEY

Predicting what may happen in the future is fraught with risk. Predicting what will happen in the future carries an even greater degree of risk. The two quotes at the opening page of this chapter, by Mr Larkin and Mr Bell, appeared very futuristic at a time when both the telephone network and air travel were very much in their infancy.

Alexander Graham Bell was born at 16 Charlotte Street, Edinburgh, Scotland on March 3rd, 1847. Thomas Larkin, the second youngest of seven children was born on July 4th, 1874, in the townland of Derrew, Ballyheane, five miles (8km) south of the town of Castlebar, County Mayo, on Ireland's west coast.

Both men, while emerging from different countries, backgrounds and societies, would proceed to share a number of common journeys in life and would ultimately revolutionize our methods of interpersonal communication through the use of a device that would be capable of transmitting the human voice over wires.

Alexander G. Bell patented and invented the telephone on March 10th, 1876. He was, along with Gardiner G. Hubbard and Thomas Sanders, a founder member of the Bell Telephone Company. Thomas Larkin enjoyed a distinguished career with the Bell Telephone Company in Pennsylvania, received much recognition and was conferred with life membership of the Telephone Pioneers of America.

For different reasons, both men were forced to emigrate from their native homelands of Scotland and Ireland, to North America, or the 'New World', as the American Continent was known at the time. Following the devastation of the Irish Potato Famine, 1845-1850, and with little prospect of securing any worthwhile future in the poverty stricken Ireland at the time, Thomas Larkin joined thousands of his fellow young men and women and emigrated, initially to Liverpool, and later Pennsylvania, U.S.A., arriving at the Port of Philadelphia on May 25th, 1899.

Chapter 1. *Before The Journey*

Research Facility - Birth Record

Uimh.	Dáta of Birth Date of Birth	Ainm Name	Gnéas Sex	Ainm, Sloinne agus Ionad Chónaithe an Athar / Name and Surname and Dwelling-Place of Father	Ainm agus Sloinne an Mháthar agus a sloinne roimh phósadh di / Name and Surname and Maiden name of Mother	Céim nó Gairm Bheatha an Athar / Rank or Profession of Father	Síniú, Cáilíocht agus Ionad Chónaithe an Fhaisnéiseora / Signature, Qualification and Residence of Informant	An Dáta a Chláraíodh / When Registered	Síniú an Chláraithora / Signature of Registrar	Ainm Baiste má tugadh é tar-éis chlarú na Breithe agus an Dáta / Baptismal Name if added after Registration of Birth and Date
112	July fourth 1874 Derreen	Thomas	Male	Michael Larkin Derreen	Mary Larkin formerly Walsh	Farmer	Mary x Larkin mark Mother Derreen	August thirteenth 1874	C. Walsh Registrar	

The birth certificate of Thomas Larkin. *Pic.: Michael Larkin.*

REGISTER OF Ballyburke NATIONAL SCHOOL. No. 40

Date of Entrance, 1885	Register Number	Pupils' Names in Full	Age of Pupil last Birth Day	Religious Denomination	Residence	Occupation or Means of Living of Parents	School	County
1.12.83	137	1 O'Malley, P. John	6	R.C	Ballyburke	Farmer	✓	
1.12.83	132	2 Cunningham Michael	7	R.C	Kelladeer	Farmer	✓	
1.12.83	157	3 O'Malley Owen	6	R.C	Cappahanane	Farmer	✓	
21.4.84	165	4 Dunne John	11	R.C	Carrabeg	Farmer	Hedge	
24.11.84	170	5 Larkin Thomas	9	R.C	Ballyburke	cottier	Ballyhane	

Roll-book pages from Ballyburke National School, showing Thomas Larkin as a nine-year-old pupil. *Pic.: Michael Larkin.*

Chapter 1. *Before The Journey*

A memorial in Clifden, close to the landing site of the pioneering transatlantic flight of Alcock and Brown.
Pic.: Michael Larkin.

At a time when travel between Ireland and North America was slowly advancing from a period of six to seven weeks, to a 'speedily' six to seven days on the ocean, A.G. Bell's prediction of "being able to have dinner in New York and breakfast in Dublin or London the following morning", was viewed as something that may happen in the distant future. When John Alcock and Arthur Brown sat down for 'dinner' in Newfoundland on the evening of Saturday, June 14th, 1919, it would be seventeen hours later before they tasted 'breakfast', not in Dublin or London, but in Clifden, County Galway. Their twin engine airplane crash-landed in a bog, at Derrigimlagh, four miles (6.5km) south of Clifden, on Sunday, June 15th, 1919. This was the first non-stop transatlantic flight between North America and Ireland. The airplane also carried 200 letters, heralding the first delivery of mail 'by air' across the Atlantic Ocean, and also the introduction of the air mail stamp.

The first official transatlantic telephone call between New York and London took place as 'recently' as January 7th, 1927. At a time when the telephone network was only in its infancy, Thomas Larkin's prediction that "the day would come when you will be able to 'see' the person who you are speaking to" appeared very futuristic. Despite much doubt, both men's predictions would come to pass.

Thomas, along with his siblings attended Ballyburke National School, which accepted its first pupils on February 1st, 1849. It was established on the site of a Chapel dating from the time of St. Patrick. Throughout the grossly overpopulated Ireland at the time, most pupils ceased attendance in primary education at 11 or 12 years of age. Only pupils from more privileged backgrounds could continue on to further education, or attend fee paying schools. Ballyburke school, like most schools in rural Ireland, was a basic two roomed structure with an open

Ballyburke National School.
Pic.: Michael Larkin.

Chapter 1. *Before The Journey*

hearth fireplace to provide heat in winter. All pupils, many who walked very long distances over difficult terrain, carried turf or wooden logs for the open fire.

In Derrew, similar to all surrounding townlands, large families, tiny thatched cabins, small fragmented farms and the constant threat of eviction for inability to pay the exorbitant rents demanded by landlords, meant there was a constant cloud of melancholy and hopelessness. However, despite this sense of gloom, there was also a great sense of closeness and neighbourliness, mainly due to the close proximity of the small farms and thatched cottages dotted throughout the hills and valleys.

A 'meitheal' or group of helpers would regularly gather and help with the saving of hay, turf, or cutting of the grain. House dances, storytelling and card playing were the main forms of entertainment. The 'American Wake' was a regular feature, when on the night before a young man or woman would emigrate to the 'New World', neighbours young and old would gather until the early hours offering words of encouragement, storytelling and generally consoling elderly parents, who most likely would never see their young sons or daughters again.

While the standard of living was extremely low most of the small farms were self sufficient, having two or three cows, one or two pigs, small numbers of sheep and some hens and geese. Remittance from family members who had already emigrated greatly assisted in raising household income.

The sale of butter and eggs to local shop keepers provided a small but essential income. In many areas, crafts such as wool spinning, weaving, crochet or basket making provided extra income.

The small farm and thatched cottage of Thomas Larkin's youth was not a lot different to most others at the time. A flag stone floor, tiny windows, a 'half-door', a large open fireplace and a cobbled laneway, leading to this white-washed cottage, would have been the residence he shared with his parents and siblings. A spring well, still visible today, provided crystal clear water for the Larkin household and neighbouring households.

A photograph of a cottage in Killawalla, County Mayo, which is typical of the cottages in existence, during Thomas Larkin's boyhood.
Pic.: Michael Larkin

Rural Life In Ireland in the 1800s

Thomas Larkin's simple early days in the townland of Derrew were a microcosm of what rural life was like in 19th century Ireland. This was a time when most people were in touch with nature, walked the roads and pathways, worked in the fields, sharpened scythes, saved the hay and picked the potatoes. It was an era when the only form of communication with the outside world was by means of a hand-written letter or occasional telegram. The taste of bacon and cabbage, the sound of a donkey or horse carts' iron-shod wheels on cobbled roadways, the smell of scented heather or new-mown hay and the sight of men and women, young and old, working in the fields was the common scene throughout rural Ireland at the time.

The Great Famine 1845-1850, caused by the failure of the potato crop, is etched in the memory of the Irish population and even deeper in the memories of the Irish diaspora, especially in the U.S.A. Prior to the potato famine, Ireland's population was over eight million people. In the aftermath of the Famine the population had dropped to just over six million. The West of Ireland, due to the poorer quality of land, suffered the greatest decline in population. The Parish of Killawalla, County Mayo, which incorporates the townland of Derrew, suffered the greatest loss proportionately in Ireland at the time, with the population dropping from 2,277 in 1841, to just 789 people by 1851 [N.U.I Maynooth National Centre For Geocomputation]. Most of the absentee landlords, who owned vast tracts of land, had little regard for tenants' welfare. Bailiffs and agents, acting on behalf of the landlord were ruthless in evicting tenants who were trying to eke out a living on uneconomic, small parcels of land.

Pictured at the Michael Davitt Museum in Straide, County Mayo, is a statue of Michael Davitt, founding member of the Land League. Note the missing arm, lost in a tragic accident in the Cotton Mills in England. *Pic.: Michael Larkin.*

Despite the decline in population, there was still far too much congestion, especially in the West of Ireland. Crop failures and poor weather throughout the 1870s led to further hardship, evictions and emigration. There was also growing agitation and anger, with meetings held to demand the return of the land to the families who worked on it. Over 15,000 people attended one such meeting in Irishtown, County Mayo, on April 20th, 1879.

Chapter 1. *Before The Journey*

An 1887 engraving of immigrants arriving in New York City. *Pic.: iStock*

The Irish National Land League was founded in the Imperial Hotel, Castlebar, on October 21st, 1879. Michael Davitt, James Daly, Charles Stewart Parnell and others addressed the large crowd. Between 1879 and 1882, hundreds more families were evicted from their small farms, due to failure to pay the exorbitant rents. This led to even greater anger, and a period that became known as the Land War.

EVICTIONS IN DERREW

Sir Robert Lynch-Blosse owned vast tracts of land in the central Mayo region at the time. Similar to the other landlords, hundreds were evicted, or forced to work for meagre days' pay on his estate. The townland of Derrew would not be immune to the wrath of this landlord. A report in the *Connaught Telegraph*, Saturday, March 11th, 1882, stated;

> *Sir R. L. Blosse was represented by his agent, bailiff and over 20 police officers, in the townland of Derrew, Ballintubber, at the eviction of the following four families; Widow Higgins, with four in family, Widow Heneghan with four in family, John Larkin with eight in family and Michael Larkin with eight in family.*

While all would return some time later to their broken down thatched cottages, the sight of policemen and bailiffs securing possession of one's home and few acres of land created much anger and resentment towards landlordism. Michael Larkin, his wife Mary and young family secured a run down, two roomed thatched cottage in the townland of Ballyburke. He worked on the estate until rent arrears were paid, before returning once again to the original small holding in Derrew.

The poet, Andrew McKenzie (1780-1839) describes his life as a cottier in a small mud-wall cabin.

> *"My mansion is a clay built cot,*
> *My whole domain a garden plot,*
> *So little straw defends the roof,*
> *Against the rain it is not proof"*

Just like thousands of other peasant farm families in rural Ireland, McKenzie, his wife and six children survived on a diet of potatoes, small amounts of grain and vegetables. Each May annual rent of 30 shillings (£1.50, $3) which was a significant figure at the time, had to be paid to ruthless landlords or their agents. This graphic description by McKenzie vividly describes the harsh and cramped living conditions, the exorbitant rents and the constant fear of eviction.

EMIGRATION

It was against this background of eviction, landlordism, and a meaningless future at home that each member of the Larkins, except Michael, the youngest, was forced to emigrate. Michael remained at home to assist his elderly parents on the small farm and seek whatever additional labouring work was available.

Having completed a basic national school education, Kate, the eldest, saw no future in remaining at home, and became

Chapter 1. *Before The Journey*

the first of the family to undertake that journey to the 'New World'. After being taken to Westport Rail Station by horse and cart, she bade a tearful farewell to her father, having already kissed and hugged her mother and younger siblings. The Midland and Great Western Steam train journey to Queenstown (Cobh) was long and painful. At each rail station stop, more and more passengers were boarding the now over-crowded train, with parents and siblings left weeping on the platform, knowing that they were unlikely to ever see their sons or daughters again. The sight of Cork City at the time was daunting to most passengers, even more daunting still was the sight of the huge ship waiting in the harbour. The one way ticket which she had purchased with some savings and a little help from her parents cost £4.10s ($25 approx) which was a considerable amount of money at the time.

On arrival in New York harbour, Ellis Island was the first port of call, where all third class or steerage passengers attempted to answer the mandatory twenty nine questions. (First and second class passengers had a much less rigorous examination). Almost immediately, Kate secured employment as a housekeeper. A number of months later, she improved her position when she became a member of the housekeeping staff of the influential Roosevelt family.

In Derrew, the sight of the postman arriving was eagerly awaited. Would there be a letter with a U.S. postmark? In one of her letters, Kate suggested that her younger sister, Maggie should join her in New York. The prospect was exciting but the cost of the one way fare was difficult to

Mary Moran (née Larkin), sister of Thomas Larkin.
Pic.: Courtesy Dan and Margaret O'Connor.

secure. Another letter arrived - this time with dollars enclosed, to help subsidise Maggie's fare to New York. Without hesitation, she was the next member of the family to undertake that same voyage as Kate had, over two years beforehand. One by one, the other members of the family made that same voyage, hoping some day to return to the land of their birth. John made the voyage and secured employment on a construction site in New York. However, writing home following hard and long working days, coupled with sub-standard accommodation, soon became a chore and in the space of a few years all contact was lost.

Mary was next to emigrate, and with the help of her sisters, she also secured employment as a housekeeper. Meanwhile, back in Derrew, as part of the Congested Districts Board's land restructuring programme, a new house was built in 1911.

By this stage Kate was married to Patrick Kearns in New York. They had no family. They made one journey back to County Mayo, with the intention of remaining at home. Kate was also anxious to see for the first time the new house in Derrew. However, after a three month stay they discovered very little had changed in rural Ireland. Despite wishing to remain at home, the prospect of an easier lifestyle in the U.S.A. over-ruled her heart's desire and both returned once more to the U.S.A. Prior to what her employer thought would be her permanent return to Ireland, she was presented with a silver plated Louis XVI cutlery set by her housekeeping supervisor and staff with the Roosevelt family.

A house typical of the bungalows constructed as part of the Congested Districts Board restructuring programme. *Pic.: Michael Larkin.*

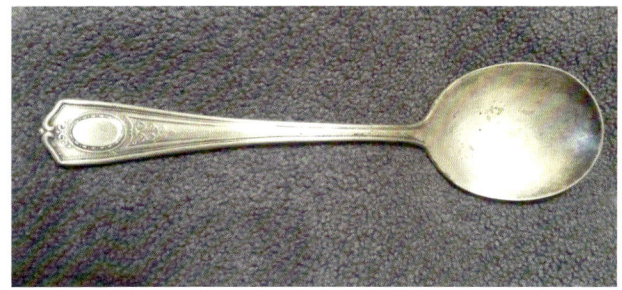

A spoon from the Louis XVI cutlery set. *Pic.: Michael Larkin.*

In August 1901, Mary married James T. Moran at St. Francis Xavier Church, 16th St. New York. Two years later, Maggie married Patrick Keeshan. Sadly she would die following childbirth at the young age of 38. It was reported at the time that she died holding the new born infant in her arms.

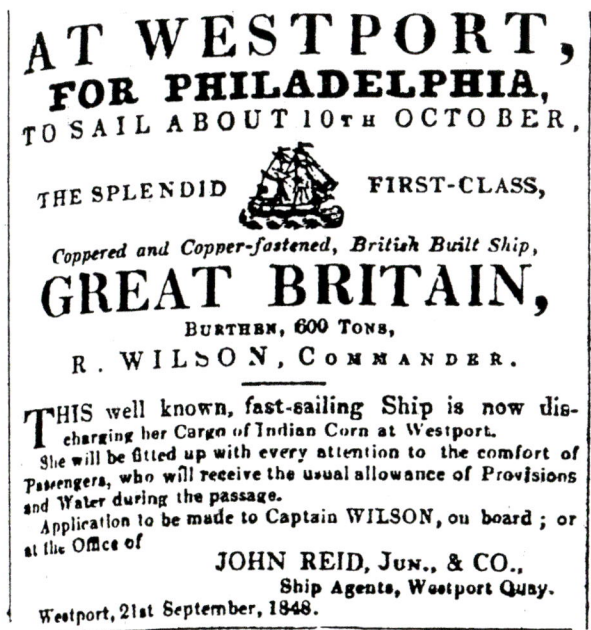

An advertisement from the Telegraph dated Autumn, 1848. *Pic.: Courtesy Mayo County Library.*

Land registry deeds, or folio, showing the former Sir Henry Lynch Blosse Estate, in ownership of the C.D.B. (Congested Districts Board). Note the date of original registration, May 24th, 1911, which was also the date of construction of a new bungalow on the Larkin farm, in the townland of Derrew.
Pic.: Michael Larkin.

2

THE JOURNEY BEGINS

Like his older siblings, Thomas would also undertake that emigrant journey. However, he initially travelled across the Irish Sea before undertaking his transatlantic voyage. Following his basic education in Ballyburke National School, he spent some time on the construction and upkeep of local roadways in Mayo. However, the work was weather-dependent, hours exceptionally long, with little prospect of any future progress. At the very young age of 16 years, he joined hundreds of young men and women at Westport rail station and boarded the mid-day Midland and Great Western Steam Train, bound for Kingstown (Dun Laoghaoire), Dublin.

Having some time to spare he decided to have one final walk around the town of Westport. His last purchase in the town was a new white shirt costing two shillings. Returning to the railway station, he took one last, lingering look back at the town that lies under the shadow of Croagh Patrick. With the new shirt added to his few meagre

James Street, Westport in the early 1900s
Pic.: courtesy Mayo County Library / National Library of Ireland.

possessions, including a Rosary Beads given to him by his mother, it was time to board the train. The train journey across the Irish midlands was slow and uncomfortable, with many stops along the way. Crossing the Irish sea at the time was also an unpleasant experience. For most passengers on board, it would have been their first time outside their native townland. In addition to passengers, most of the boats carried livestock, grain and other farm produce. Many of the boats were overcrowded, deck

Chapter 2. *The Journey Begins*

The Swainson Birley and Company Cotton Mills in Preston, Lancashire, England, 1835, was typical of the Cotton Mills of the time. The seven storey high mill building was 475 feet in length and had 660 windows. *Pic.: Shutterstock.*

passengers exposed to all types of weather, with many passengers ill-prepared for such a journey. Liverpool at this time was one of the busiest ports in the United Kingdom. It was also a major gateway port for emigrants travelling to other parts of the world. Thomas immediately secured employment in one of the many warehouses along the docks.

Some time later, he followed in the footsteps of the highly respected Mayo man Michael Davitt, founder of the National Land League, and gained employment in the L. Whitaker and Sons Cotton Mills. While Thomas was happy to have secured employment in the mills, his love for the open countryside led him to seeking farm work. Some time later he became what we would today term a Farm Manager, on one of the many large farms in the Lancashire region.

Although very well respected in the Lancashire region, and regarded as a 'good contact' for many Irish immigrants arriving daily in search of work, he was becoming more and more interested in securing a better future in the 'New World'. Throughout Britain and Ireland at the time, colourful posters and banners were being displayed on shop fronts, lamp posts, street corners, etc., proclaiming 'Great opportunities in the New World'. Were the posters telling the truth, he wondered? Reports and letters were also being received, outlining how many who had crossed the Atlantic Ocean had prospered and 'made a fortune' in the New World.

"I'm goin' far across the foam, to far Amerikay,

There's gold and jewels a plenty,

For the poor and for the gentry,

So instead of diggin' praties,

I'll be diggin' lumps of gold"

Muirsheen Durkin - a popular folk song dating from the 1850s, recorded by many artists.

Songs such as Muirsheen Durkin glamorised the notion that all Irish immigrants in 'far Amerikay' were 'diggin' lumps of gold'.

Throughout the months of February, March and April 1899, despite being well-respected by his employer, Thomas was becoming increasingly unsettled in Lancashire. Many of his new acquaintances and friends were being influenced with the prospect of 'making it big' in the U.S.A. or Canada. Pat Dolan, a friend who Thomas had earlier assisted in securing employment in Lancashire, had already crossed the Atlantic and according to Mr Dolan's brother, who was a recent arrival in Liverpool, he was "doing very well for himself" in Philadelphia. Whether it was true or not, 'doing very well for himself' sounded good. And so, the decision was made. Thomas purchased his one-way ticket on May 10th, 1899 to embark on his voyage of discovery across the Atlantic to the 'New World'.

Chapter 2. *The Journey Begins*

SS 'Etruria', Pierhead, Liverpool, 1890-1910 Pic.: Alamy

CROSSING THE ATLANTIC

By the late 1800s competition amongst rival shipping companies on the North Atlantic was intense. While conditions on board had improved from the 'coffin ships' of the post famine era, the length of time spent on the ocean was still very weather dependent. Many of the smaller boats and ships spent six or seven weeks at sea during the mid 1800s. With his £7 ($35) one way ticket in hand, he boarded the S.S. Etruria, bound for Philadelphia.

Most passengers on board had mixed emotions. Many were delighted to be getting away to a 'New World', others resented having been forced to emigrate, while many more remained silent, keeping their thoughts to themselves. However, there was also some singing and dancing on board, which would help erase memories of hardship at home.

"I'm bidding farewell to the land of my youth,
And the home I'm leaving behind,
And the mountains grand 'round my own native land,
I'm bidding them all farewell, with an aching heart,
I'll bid them adieu, for tomorrow, I sail far away,
O'er the raging foam, to seek a home,
On the shores of Amerikay".

(Wolfe Tones 1976)

Philadelphia Here I Come

Thomas Larkin was, by now, firmly focused on discovering the 'New World' and silently wishing for his American dream to become a reality. In many ways, his wish was similar to that of the young man in the play by Brian Friel 'Philadelphia Here I Come', 1964, which chronicles an Irish immigrant's journey from the West of Ireland to Philadelphia who is forever gripped in the nostalgia of home and the endless promise of fulfilling his American dream.

The first sightings of land, through the morning mists, were greeted with sighs of relief, shrieks of joy and nervous excitement. As the ship entered Delaware Bay, with the State of New Jersey on the right, Delaware on the left, and the tall multi-storey buildings of Philadelphia stretching into the skyline, all on board nervously awaited stepping onto American soil.

Philadelphia docklands were a hive of activity, the port was second to New York in terms of passenger and cargo movement at the time. Colourful posters, job advertisements promising 'great opportunities', 'work available', 'create a new future', etc., were everywhere. Yet, despite the many advertisements, it became apparent to Thomas that there were queues of people waiting to be hired. Doubts began to re-surface in his mind regarding his decision to leave Liverpool. Many years later, he stated "If I had the fare to return to Liverpool at the time, I would have done so". However, he did secure employment with

Chapter 2. *The Journey Begins*

8th and Market Street Philadelphia in the early 1900s.
Pic.: courtesy of Free Library of Philadelphia/Lit Bros. Building/11193.

Chapter 2. *The Journey Begins*

Thomas Larkin's American passport. *Pic.: Michael Larkin.*

one of the many construction companies close to the port. Within a short time, his supervisory experience from Liverpool would prove useful. He was promoted to office and wages clerk with the firm. Most Irish immigrants secured work through 'word of mouth', or other informal contacts. Nevertheless, there was much social unrest and tension, with many industries adopting a 'hire and fire' policy, resulting in most unskilled Irish immigrants remaining on the breadline. Posters continued to be displayed on lamp posts, shop windows and other hoardings, seeking workers. However, most of the work was not in the Philadelphia region, the promise of 'gold' was in West Pennsylvania and the American Mid-West.

23

*"The day is coming when telephone wires
will be connected to houses,
much like water and gas,
so that friends will be able to converse with each other
without leaving home".
(Alexander G. Bell)*

3

THE DEVELOPMENT OF THE TELEPHONE

At the time of Thomas Larkin's arrival in the U.S.A. the 'most modern form of communication in the world' - the telephone, was just over 20 years in existence, following its invention in Boston by Alexander Graham Bell in 1876.

BEFORE THE TELEPHONE

Following the deaths of Alexander's brothers Edward (19) and Melville (25) from tuberculosis, with Alexander himself also threatened, the entire Bell family emigrated from Scotland to Brantford, Ontario where they purchased a 13 acre (5.2 ha) farm. Alexander later travelled south to Boston where he was employed as a teacher for the deaf. He also established a small laboratory, where along with others, he conducted experiments on the transmission of messages over wires.

On the basic hierarchy of needs, man's need for food, warmth and shelter are deemed the most basic. The ability and need to communicate not only interpersonally but also to receive and transmit 'news', or other happenings, either within one's own community, neighbourhood, country or internationally, in the shortest space of time, is also deemed a basic need nowadays.

From the dawn of civilization, humans communicated with each other, firstly through the most basic vocal sounds, which later evolved to form words and later still meaningful sentences. Man also communicated through the medium of art, signs, scrolls, writings and letters. Small settlements, which would later become villages, towns or great cities, developed their own systems of communications. Minor dirt tracks gradually became pathways, which over time evolved into a network of roadways. People walked huge distances, over mountainous terrain and vast tracts of countryside. They trained horses to travel longer distances, wagons, log boats, currachs, barges and ships were built to discover many 'new worlds', and deliver messages to faraway lands. As the centuries rolled by, many experiments, developments and inventions were

Chapter 3. *The Development of the Telephone*

Samuel F. B. Morse (1791-1872), painter and inventor of an electric telegraph.
Pic.: Shutterstock

Michael Faraday, inventor of the electric dynamo.
Pic.: Shutterstock

Thomas Edison, inventor of the electric light bulb.
Pic.: Shutterstock

Guglielmo Marconi, credited with the refinement and development of long distance radio transmission.
Pic.: Shutterstock

John Logie Baird inventor of the television.
Pic.: Geroge Grantham Bain collection at Library of Congress. Public Domain.

undertaken by scientists, physicists, mathematicians and others, in pursuit of improvements in communication.

In the early eighteenth century, Benjamin Franklin carried out experiments in electrical conduction. However, it was Michael Faraday who invented the electric dynamo in 1831. This formed the basis for electric motor technology. In 1879, Thomas Edison invented and patented the electric light bulb.

In parallel with the development of electricity, experiments were also being undertaken in the fields of communication. In 1844 a telegraph line was installed between Washington D.C. and Baltimore, using Samuel F.B. Morse's key and receiver system. This would become known as the Morse Code and he successfully applied for patent rights in 1849.

In the late 1800s much research was undertaken in the transmission of signals by means of electromagnetic waves. This paved the way for the wireless, or radio as it would become known. Heinrich R. Hertz performed the first transmission using electromagnetic waves, but Guglielmo Marconi (1874 – 1937) is credited with further refinement and development of long distance radio transmission.

In 1907 the opening of the Marconi Radio Station in Clifden paved the way for the first transatlantic radio messages. In 1909, Marconi shared the Nobel Prize in physics with Karl Ferdinand Brawn 'In recognition of their contribution to wireless telegraphy'.

The first radio broadcast for entertainment was transmitted on December 24th, 1906, from Brant Rock, Massachusetts by Reginald A. Fessender (1866-1932). However, the first commercial licensed radio station broadcast was made by Radio K.D.K.A. Pittsburgh, which went 'on air', November 2nd, 1920. In Ireland, 2RN, later to be renamed Radio Éireann, began broadcasting on January 1st, 1926.

Throughout the early 1900s developments in what would become known as television began to appear. The terms used at the time were 'images over wires'. On January 26th, 1926, Scottish inventor John Logie Baird demonstrated what is believed to be the first television transmission in history.

From 1905 until 1922, this remote site in Derrigimlagh Bog, near Clifden, County Galway, was where Guglielmo Marconi successfully completed the first commercial wireless transmission of Morse code across the Atlantic.
The two rusted pieces of metal (above) are all that remain from the giant alternators which powered the Marconi radio station - note the Marconi name cut into the sheet metal.
Pic.: Michael Larkin.

Chapter 3. *The Development of the Telephone*

Alexander Graham Bell (1847-1922) at age 18 in Elgin, Scotland prior to his emigration to Canada in 1870. *Pic.: Shutterstock.*

Alexander Graham Bell pictured in his latter years. *Pic.: Pixabay*

INVENTION OF THE TELEPHONE

> On March 7th 1876 A.G. Bell was issued with his U.S. patent, bearing the number 174,465, for the invention of 'a device' to carry spoken words over a wire.

Following his move to Boston, Bell taught in a number of schools for the deaf, throughout Massachusetts. He established a school to train teachers in 'vocal physiology and the mechanics of speech'. Two of his pupils happened to be the son and daughter of wealthy businessmen. One was the five year old son of Thomas Sanders, a leather merchant in Salem, the other was Mabel Hubbard, daughter of Gardiner Greene Hubbard, an attorney and President of the National Geographic Society. Thomas Sanders and Gardiner Greene Hubbard offered to support Bell financially in his pursuit of his dream to pioneer a device to transmit the human voice over a wire. The three men agreed to form a company and share any profits equally from Bell's experiments. This company was to be the foundation of what would become the Bell Telephone Company of America. Gardiner G. Hubbard was President, Thomas Sanders became Treasurer, with Bell becoming 'Chief Electrician'. Bell continued teaching, conducting most of his research and experiments at night over Charles Williams' electrical shop at 109 Court Street, Boston.

Mr Williams assigned a young Thomas Watson to assist Bell. Progress was slow, with many disappointments along the way. Hubbard would later admit that he was sceptical of spoken words ever being transmitted over a wire.

Sanders was also becoming impatient and many of his friends labelled his investment in the company as 'Sanders Folly'. However, Bell and Watson were making some progress, initially with muffled voice sounds over a wire. After much experimentation and refinement the muffled sounds became more and more audible.

> Following the accidental spilling of acid, Bell called out -
> "Mr Watson, come here, I want you".
> Watson heard him over the wires they were working on and ran to his assistance.
> This was the first time a message of coherent words was transmitted over a wire, heralding the introduction of the world's first working telephone.

Many refinements and modifications followed. Posters and notices started to appear urging the public to attend demonstrations outlining 'this new modern means of communication'. However, the general public were not impressed and Bell and his investors were starting to lose hope. The Boston Post carried a headline -

'well informed people know that it is impossible to transmit the voice over wires, even if it were possible, it would be of no practical use'.

Chapter 3. *The Development of the Telephone*

PHILADELPHIA U. S. AMERICA — MAY 10TH to NOVEMBER 10TH 1876.

MAIN EXHIBITION BUILDING.

1776 — INTERNATIONAL EXHIBITION — 1876

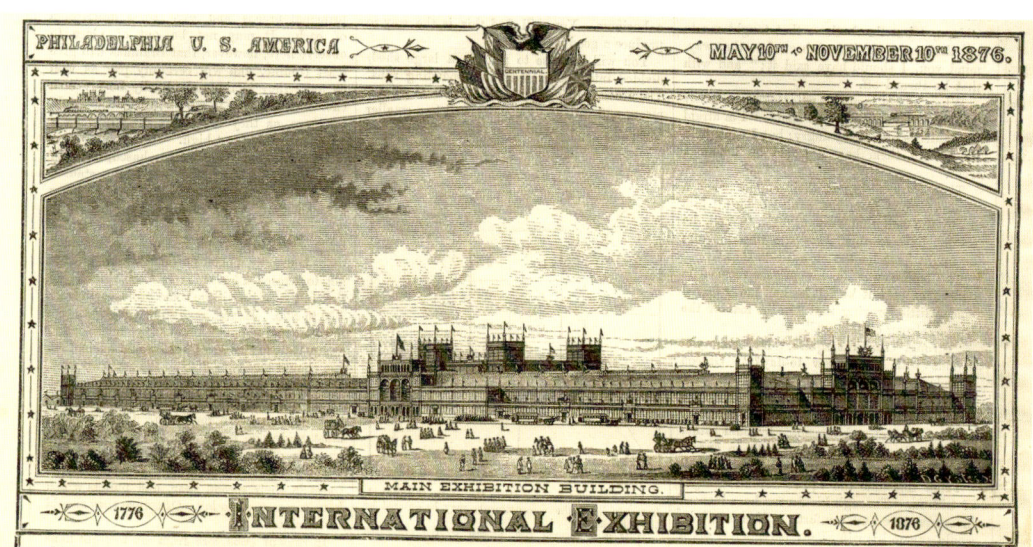

In celebration of the signing of the Declaration of Independence, which took place in Philadelphia, July 4, 1776 (one hundred years ago), the United States have arranged to hold an International Exhibition. The buildings are situated in Fairmount Park, Philadelphia, on the banks of the Schuylkill River, and the space reserved for exhibition purposes is 450 acres. The area under cover is no less than 75 acres, or three times the space covered in the Exhibition held in London in 1862. The buildings are six in number, three of which will be permanent structures. The Main Exhibition Building is 1,880 feet in length by 464 in width. The Art Gallery, 365 feet by 210; the Machinery Hall, 1,402 feet by 360, with an annexe 208 feet by 210; the Horticultural Hall, 383 feet by 193. The ground covered by the Agricultural Building is a parallelogram of 465 by 630 feet.

The Art Gallery, erected by the State of Pennsylvania, is a structure of granite and brick, surmounted by a dome of glass and iron.

The Agricultural Building, made of wood and glass, will contain the many wonderful farming implements for which the Americans are famed.

The Horticultural Building has been erected by the city of Philadelphia, the chief materials

THE AGRICULTURAL BUILDING.

Details of the International Exhibition held in Philadelphia in 1876. The scale of this event was enormous as can be seen in this picture, showing only two of the several buildings used to house specific expositions.

The exhibition and demonstration by Alexander G. Bell of the world's first working telephone, captivated the attention of the thousands of people in attendance.

Pic.: iStock

30

Chapter 3. *The Development of the Telephone*

To celebrate the centenary of the signing of the Declaration of Independence, the Centennial Exposition World Fair was held in Philadelphia throughout the summer of 1876. The scale of the exposition was enormous (see opposite page) with the main building covering an area of over 20 acres (8.5 hectares). New inventions were on display including sewing machines, typewriters, stoves, agricultural equipment and steam engines. Almost at the point of desperation, Bell and Watson decided to attend and exhibit their invention.

This decision proved to be a masterstroke, with many sceptics now witnessing that the device actually worked. Following the exposition, Bell and Watson travelled throughout the United States, with increasing numbers of people and influential businessmen attending events to witness the telephone in operation. As the number of telephones began to increase, a 'central office', or exchange was required. The first telephone exchange was opened on January 28th, 1878, in New Haven, Connecticut.

Many other milestones would follow. On July 1st, 1881, the world's first international telephone call was made between the city of St. Stephen, New Brunswick, Canada and Calais, Maine, U.S.A. The first long distance coast to coast call was made by A. G. Bell in New York to his assistant, Thomas Watson, in San Francisco on January 25th, 1915. The first transatlantic telephone call between New York and London took place on January 7th, 1927. In 1929, President Herbert Hoover had the first telephone installed at his desk in the Oval Office in the White House, Washington D.C.

President Herbert Hoover,
31st President of the United States of America.
Pic.: Library of Congress (public domain)

While Alexander G. Bell deserves enormous credit for patenting and inventing the very first telephone, without Sanders, Hubbard, Vail, Watson and many other pioneers, including Thomas Larkin, the network would not have expanded throughout the U.S.A.

Bell's Other Achievements

"The achievement of one goal should be the starting point of another" - A.G. Bell.

Never a man to stand still, Bell was granted several more U.S. patents for further innovation in telecommunication, including a patent for the invention of the Photophone in December 1880. The Photophone, which was the precursor of today's fiber optical communications, allowed the transmission of speech on a beam of light. This new innovation in communications resulted in the Photophone becoming the world's earliest known wireless transmission of the human voice, at least twenty years ahead of the first spoken radio transmission. In his latter years, Bell deemed this invention as "my greatest invention … even ahead of the telephone". In one of his many interviews he stated "we can only imagine what the future of this invention is to be … discoveries will be made by the Photophone which are undreamed of right now".

Alexander G. Bell died at his home in Nova Scotia on August 2nd, 1922. Following his death, two days later all telephone services throughout the entire continent of North America were suspended for one minute in his honour at the precise moment when his body was lowered into the grave.

Today, very few could dispute that U.S. patent number 174,465 is still widely believed to be the most valuable patent ever issued.

THE CELL PHONE AND TODAY'S PIONEERS

American innovator and Marconi prize recipient Martin (Marty) Cooper described one of the most dangerous things he ever did was to cross a busy New York street while making a telephone call. Curious onlookers and pedestrians asked "What are you doing? Who are you talking to?" His reply was "I've just invented the world's first cell phone and I'm making a call!". The date was April 3rd, 1973. However it would be another ten years before the cellular or mobile phone would become commercially available. I had the pleasure of meeting with Mr Cooper some time ago, and he recounted how primitive, by today's standards, that first cell phone was. It weighed 2.5 pounds (1.1kg), measured 9in X 5in (23cm X 13cm) and was shaped like a brick with an aerial.

In many ways, the rapid growth of email and the internet, personal computers, smartphones, digital media, etc. mirrors the changes in our methods of communication, much as the telephone did in its early days, following its invention in 1876.

Bill Gates and Paul Allen, co - founders of Microsoft 1975, Steve Jobs and Steve Wozniak, co-founders of Apple 1976, Mark Zuckerberg, Facebook 2004 and many other innovators in the field of advanced technology are today's equivalent of Alexander G. Bell and the Telephone Pioneers of the past.

THE EARLY YEARS OF THE TELEPHONE AND POST OFFICE IN IRELAND

It's impossible to comprehend nowadays, but before an individual could make a call from a phone kiosk, they would first have to be 'connected' by a telephone operator, who would then inform the caller to insert the appropriate fee in coins, before commencement of the call.

The Post Offices throughout Ireland are interlinked with the history of the telephone network, maintaining a precious link with the Irish diaspora overseas. Prior to the arrival of the telephone, the telegraph or a telegram in the form of a typed message conveyed the delivery of good or sad news over long distances. The provision of a telephone network during a time of economic hardship was not a priority for the Irish Government in the early 1900s. In addition the prohibitive cost of installing a telephone was beyond the reach of most families. There was also a strong suspicion that telephone operators would 'listen in' on private conversations. In many respects the gradual roll-out of the telephone service in Ireland reflected a similar pattern to its roll-out in the U.S.A. many years earlier.

The Department of Posts and Telegraphs (P&T) was responsible for Ireland's postal and telecommunications services from 1924-1984. The first telephone kiosk in Ireland was installed in Dublin in May 1925. Gradually, more kiosks appeared at rail stations, post offices and street junctions in major towns and cities throughout the country.

Around this time, whilst some small businesses and shop keepers already had the telephone installed, for most day to day survival was a first priority, rather than visualising the wonders of modern telecommunication systems in far away America. Even by his own admission, Mr Gerard Boland T.D. who was Minister for Posts and Telegraphs from 1933 to 1936 did not own a telephone at the time.

While the occasional radio, or 'wireless' was starting to appear in rural Ireland, it would be December 23rd 1947

Telephone kiosk located close to the village of Killawalla, in County Mayo.
Pic.: Michael Larkin

Chapter 3. *The Development of the Telephone*

An old wireless radio from the Larkin homestead
Pic.: Michael Larkin

before the first transistor radio was invented by Bell Laboratories. However, it would be 1954 before the transistor radio went into commercial production. Throughout the 1950s, the Rural Electrification Programme delivered electricity to most of rural Ireland. Labour Deputy Jim Larkin (Jnr.) stated in March 1945: "We are going to put into the homes of our people in rural Ireland, a light which will light in their minds, as well as their homes". In Killawalla and surrounding townlands electricity was first 'switched on', on December 8th 1954.

Almost all rural communities had a local post office. The post office in Ballyheane was operated by the McGovern family and in Killawalla by the Walsh family, who provided an uninterrupted service since 1934, until its closure in December 2016. The telephone installed in Killawalla Post Office in 1952 was one of the first in the region.

A 'P&T' (Post & Telegraph) letterbox, located close to Ballintubber Abbey, County Mayo.
Pic.: Michael Larkin

4

THOMAS LARKIN, FROM PHILADELPHIA TO PITTSBURGH

The mammoth Philadelphia Centennial World Exposition was held in 1876 to commemorate the signing of the Declaration of Independence one hundred years earlier. It showcased the latest innovations and inventions in science, technology, manufacturing and labour saving devices imaginable. Now, over twenty five years later, Thomas was employed in the Fairmount Park area, along the banks of the Schuylkill River, the site of the Centennial Exposition. Many of his more senior co-workers had either attended, or worked on the construction of the giant exposition hall. One of those co-workers, who was a distant relation of Thomas Sanders, described, in a conversation with Thomas Larkin, how he witnessed firsthand Alexander Graham Bell demonstrating his new invention to thousands of stunned onlookers. This conversation would prove to be the catalyst that would take Thomas Larkin on the next phase of his journey. While he had secured regular work in Philadelphia at the time, the conversation with his co-worker regarding the marvel of the telephone kept 'ringing' in his ears. The Bell Telephone Company of Pennsylvania was also seeking workers of all grades – but not in the Philadelphia region. The jobs on offer were in Western Pennsylvania and the greater American Mid-West. Hundreds of Irish and other immigrants were already moving westwards at this time. Coal mining, railroad and canal construction attracted many Irish to the reasonably well paid but physically demanding work projects. The copper mines in Butte, Montana, also attracted many Irish immigrants. Ironically, much of the copper from this mine was being used in the manufacture of cable for the expanding telephone and electrical network.

Thomas was seriously contemplating: should he walk away from the relative comfort of Philadelphia, or take a gamble by riding out west to Pittsburgh? He was also mindful of the time of his arrival in Philadelphia when the promised 'great opportunities' were difficult to find.

The prospect of sitting an interview in Pittsburgh for an industry that he was curious about, but not very familiar

Chapter 4. *Philadelphia to Pittsburgh*

The women's waiting room from the Pittsburgh & Lake Erie Railroad Station is excellently preserved in the impressive Grand Concourse restaurant, in Pittsburgh's Station Square. This station was a major terminus for the thousands of immigrants arriving daily to work in the coal mining, steel and glass industry in the greater Pittsburgh region throughout the early 1900s. Thanks to the efforts of the Pittsburgh History & Landmarks Foundation, the sounds and smells of giant steam engines from the past have given way to the aroma and ambience of fine dining today.

Pic: Michael Larkin

with, was also a big gamble. However his curiosity won out with the prospect of a new beginning in a new city further west. There was to be no more hesitation. Decision made, this time instead of 'Philadelphia, Here I Come', it was to be 'Pittsburgh, Here I Come'. On a Monday morning, with his $8 one way ticket in his hand, he boarded the west bound steam train at Broad Street Rail Station, which would take him the Union Station Pittsburgh.

At the time of his journey, the railroads had overtaken canal barges and stagecoach wagons in the transport of passengers and goods. When the Pennsylvania railroad was opened in 1854, the Pittsburgh Daily Morning Post stated;

There are people now living in Pittsburgh who have spent a full week travelling to reach Philadelphia. The same persons can now travel the same distance, between sunrise and sunset, on a summer's day, without fatigue.

The Pennsylvania railroad traverses both rugged and fertile terrain, along the banks of the Susquehanna River and through the Allegheny Mountain Range. In the words of the Stonewall Jackson song 'Smoke Along the Track', Thomas Larkin was now leaving Philadelphia behind, as the steam train made its journey westwards towards Pittsburgh.

After a 13-hour journey, the steam train eventually screeched to a halt in Union Station, Pittsburgh. Amongst the hundreds arriving in Pittsburgh that evening, this was a new world to Thomas Larkin. His first priority was to secure a bed for the night. Very soon, he noticed a sign which read: 'lodging house ahead, rooms 50c per night'.

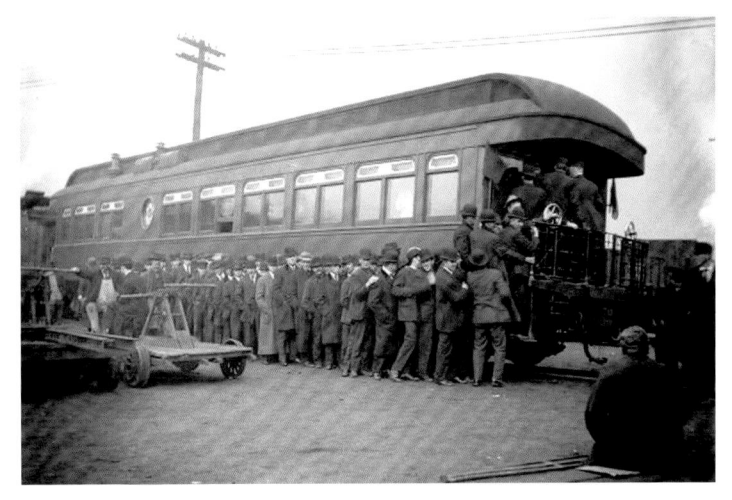

Pittsburgh and Lake Erie Railroad pay car. Hundreds of men eagerly await payment at the end of a work roster during the construction of the Pittsburgh & Lake Erie railroad.
Pic.: Courtesy University of Pittsburgh Library & Archives Centre.

On that dimly lit street, he climbed the steps, knocked on the wood panelled door of the lodging house. The creaking door opened . . . but the landlady's 'greeting' was not what he expected: "Welcome to hell", she said. "There's only one bed left, if you want it", was her next utterance. Tired, weary and reluctant to walk any further, Thomas accepted the last bed available. He twisted and turned in his sleep that night, desperately trying to figure out what was meant by the "welcome to hell" 'greeting'. Was this a house of ill repute? Was this one 'hell' of a city?

DAYBREAK IN PITTSBURGH

Whatever about the 'greeting' the previous night, the breakfast next morning was wholesome. It was now time to discover Pittsburgh – or more importantly, 'discover' the

Bell Telephone Headquarters, where, according to the posters, hundreds of new jobs were available. On arrival at the building, he took his place in the queue. Everybody in that queue had the same ambition – hopeful of securing work with the company. There was some informal banter, however most remained silent, many staring straight ahead. By now Thomas was almost at the front – not an Irishman in sight, and definitely no sign of a familiar 'Mayo' face! There was little point in turning back now. Then the clerk shouted "Next". After a very brief conversation, Thomas was handed a three page application form, with the clerk saying "Complete this application form and come back tomorrow ... Next".

It was at this point that he realized why some strong, able bodied men were leaving the counter with a demoralised look and a shake of their heads. He also realized that the basic education he had received in Ballyburke National School and his attendance at night school in Philadelphia would prove useful after all. The Bell company expected a basic level of literacy and numeracy skills from each prospective employee. Despite having a strong work ethic, most Irish immigrants avoided work which required a written 'test', form filling etc. With the application form securely tucked inside his green tweed jacket, he had some time on his hands before returning to the lodging house. Through the haze in the distance, he noticed a truck and a gang of workmen. Coming closer, the writing on the side of the truck read 'Bell Telephone Company of Pennsylvania'. The men were on lunch break at the time, so he summoned up the courage and stopped for a chat. None of the gang of nine or ten men appeared to be Irish, but they had a good command of the English language. At this point Thomas wasn't concerned where the men were from, he was more interested in finding out if the Bell Company was a good employer. The men, especially one man who appeared to be a supervisor, spoke proudly of the company. One of the men said "see that building over there, that's the Bell Headquarters, go down there and ask them about becoming a telephone lineman". The supervisor's voice then shouted "back to work, lads". The term 'telephone lineman' sounded interesting. Thomas had never heard that term before. Would the three-page form in the sealed envelope mention that term? He resisted the temptation to open the brown envelope, until he returned to the lodging house.

On this occasion the landlady's greeting was a little more friendly, possibly aware that Thomas might become a more permanent tenant. "Did you find any work?" she asked. He referred to his attendance at the Bell office earlier, and that he had also spoken to some of the telephone workmen. "If you get work with Bell, you'll be well looked after", she replied. This was the 'second recommendation' and made Thomas all the more determined to follow his dream.

THE BROWN ENVELOPE

Following dinner that evening, and on reaching an agreement with the landlady to remain at this address for at least one week, it was time to open the brown envelope. The typewritten three pages were a combination of job description and application forms, with the words 'Bell Telephone Company of Pennsylvania' in bold print. One quote, Thomas would later recall, stood out from the rest of the 'small print'.

'At Bell, we don't make promises we can't keep, we keep promises we make'.

Many of the job titles on the form sounded strange – telephone installer, lineman, splicer, cable runner, trencher, cross arm fixer, etc. The form requested basic details such as name, next of kin, nationality, permanent address etc. Hopeful that the lodging house was situated in a 'respectable' part of town, he gave this address as his 'permanent place of residence'.

The following morning, once again grey and overcast, he walked the two miles to the Bell office with the completed forms. Again there was a queue of men seeking work. He was directed to another counter, the clerk carefully scrutinised the forms and said "You'll be hearing from us inside four days". FOUR DAYS, Thomas thought to himself. Worse still, four working days meant six days in total, taking the weekend into account, before he would receive a reply.

Walking alongside the H.J. Heinz office, he noticed a sign which read 'workers wanted on a daily basis to pick fruit and vegetables'. Henry J. Heinz established the company in Pittsburgh in 1869 to manufacture a range of products, including its iconic Heinz Tomato Ketchup. While there was absolutely no guarantee, he still remained hopeful of a favourable reply from Bell. In the meantime he obtained

A horse drawn Heinz delivery cart in the H. J. Heinz History Center, Pittsburgh. Henry John Heinz founded a small company from his little garden outside Pittsburgh, selling tomatoes and pickles in 1869. Today, Pittsburgh remains the headquarters for the giant H. J. Heinz Corporation.
Pic.: Michael Larkin, taken at the H. J. Heinz History Center Pittsburgh

casual work with the Heinz Company. Returning to his 'permanent address', he enquired from the landlady the time of mail delivery. "Eleven O'Clock", she replied, "but it's usually later on a Monday". This was not what he wanted to hear, however it was now time to count down the hours until the 'later' mail arrived on Monday.

Just before midday, the eagerly awaited letter arrived, requesting him to attend the Bell office the next day to undergo a physical examination. If the medical report indicated 'good health and fitness' he was to report the following morning for the position of trainee lineman. This would become the next chapter in his life, and lead to a long and distinguished career with the Bell Telephone Company.

Chapter 4. *Philadelphia to Pittsburgh*

THE LINEMAN

The term 'trainee lineman' was a misnomer. Apart from a very small amount of theoretical training from day one, for Thomas Larkin and other 'trainee' linemen it was to be on-the-job training and work, work, work. While the network continued to expand throughout the U.S.A., there was also much resistance. Many parents objected on the grounds that the role of 'messenger boy' would become extinct. The telephone was also expensive and considered an unnecessary luxury. Direct selling, demonstrations and newspaper advertisements were used to encourage the public and business community to purchase a telephone. It's difficult to comprehend in today's highly connected world that instructions were necessary in the correct methods of receiving and making a call. At the time, the telephone comprised of two parts - a mouthpiece and receiver, in addition to wires and cables. It would be 1930 before the first combined mouthpiece and receiver was manufactured. Looking back on that occasion when Thomas stopped to speak with the gang of telephone men during their lunch break, little did he realize that one day he would also become a lineman, supervisor and a valued employee with the Bell Telephone Company of Pennsylvania. Famous names such as Heinz, Carnegie, Kaufmanns, Mellon, Rooney, Westinghouse, etc. were well established in Pittsburgh at the time. Although some of those names have disappeared from the limelight, many still retain a significant presence in the U.S.A. with some being well known household names throughout the world.

Most industries and businesses at the time were ruthless in their pursuit of profits. This was especially the case in the coal mining and iron and steel industries, which had little regard for health or safety and a 'hire and fire' policy being the order of the day. However, there were exceptions. Henry J. Heinz made it his policy to meet and greet each employee. Similarly, senior management with Bell were encouraged to maintain high standards, while at the same time appreciate both customers and employees.

Though Thomas Larkin would remain single throughout his life, he had a broad circle of friends and acquaintances within the Bell company and throughout the West Pennsylvania / North East Ohio regions. He resided on Pittsburgh's South Side for most of his working life. This region of Pittsburgh was home to thousands of immigrants from Germany, France, Italy, Eastern Europe and sizeable numbers from Scotland and Ireland. Most were employed in the glass and steel industry. Construction and other outdoor workers were exposed to extreme temperatures, which could range from a low of -13 F (-25 C) to a high of 95 F (35 C). He recounted later "if you spat in Pittsburgh on the coldest winter's day, it would be frozen before it hit the ground!" While the Bell company supplied clothing and footwear to linemen and other outdoor workers, today they would be deemed awkward and heavy. Headgear was only worn as a protection from the elements. The first 'hard hat' was patented by E.D. Bullard, California in 1919. It was simply a boiled canvas hat, covered with tar and allowed to 'cure' in the sun. The first time hard hats became mandatory was during the construction of the Hoover Dam on the Colorado River in 1931.

While the Bell company demanded high productivity from each of its employees, regardless of rank, the company in return was respectful of each employee's contribution and offered many internal promotional opportunities. In fact, many members of senior management commenced their careers at junior level and gained experience in various roles within the company structure.

Thomas Larkin commenced his career as a lineman, spending many years in that role. He also climbed the career ladder and served for a number of years at supervisory and managerial level. The number of serious work related accidents and deaths in the construction, railroad and mining sectors in the U.S.A. was very high at the time. The job of lineman was also considered dangerous, with a higher than average number of accidents and fatalities. Thomas had an unblemished record as a lineman and received a special merit 'No lost time in accidents' award. While there was little regard for the health and safety of workers in American industry at the time, he spearheaded many initiatives and prioritized the need for a greater degree of safety among linemen and other manual workers within the telephone industry. As a supervisor, perhaps ahead of his time, he constantly emphasised the words 'Remember - Safety First' to teams of workers as they commenced their daily work rotas. As his career progressed with the telephone company Thomas received much acknowledgement and recognition for his

This copper cup was presented to Thomas Larkin at a ceremony in the Bell Telephone Company Headquarters in Pittsburgh, in recognition of his unblemished record as a dedicated employee. The name T. LARKIN is engraved beneath the embossed, circular 'Bell Telephone Company of Pennsylvania' emblem. *Pic.: Michael Larkin.*

role in the delivery of the telephone network in the American Mid-West. He was conferred with Life Membership of the Telephone Pioneers of America at a ceremony in the American Telegraph and Telephone (AT&T) Headquarters in New York. At the time Life Membership was only granted to employees who had given long and distinguished service and excelled in their career

Chapter 4. *Philadelphia to Pittsburgh*

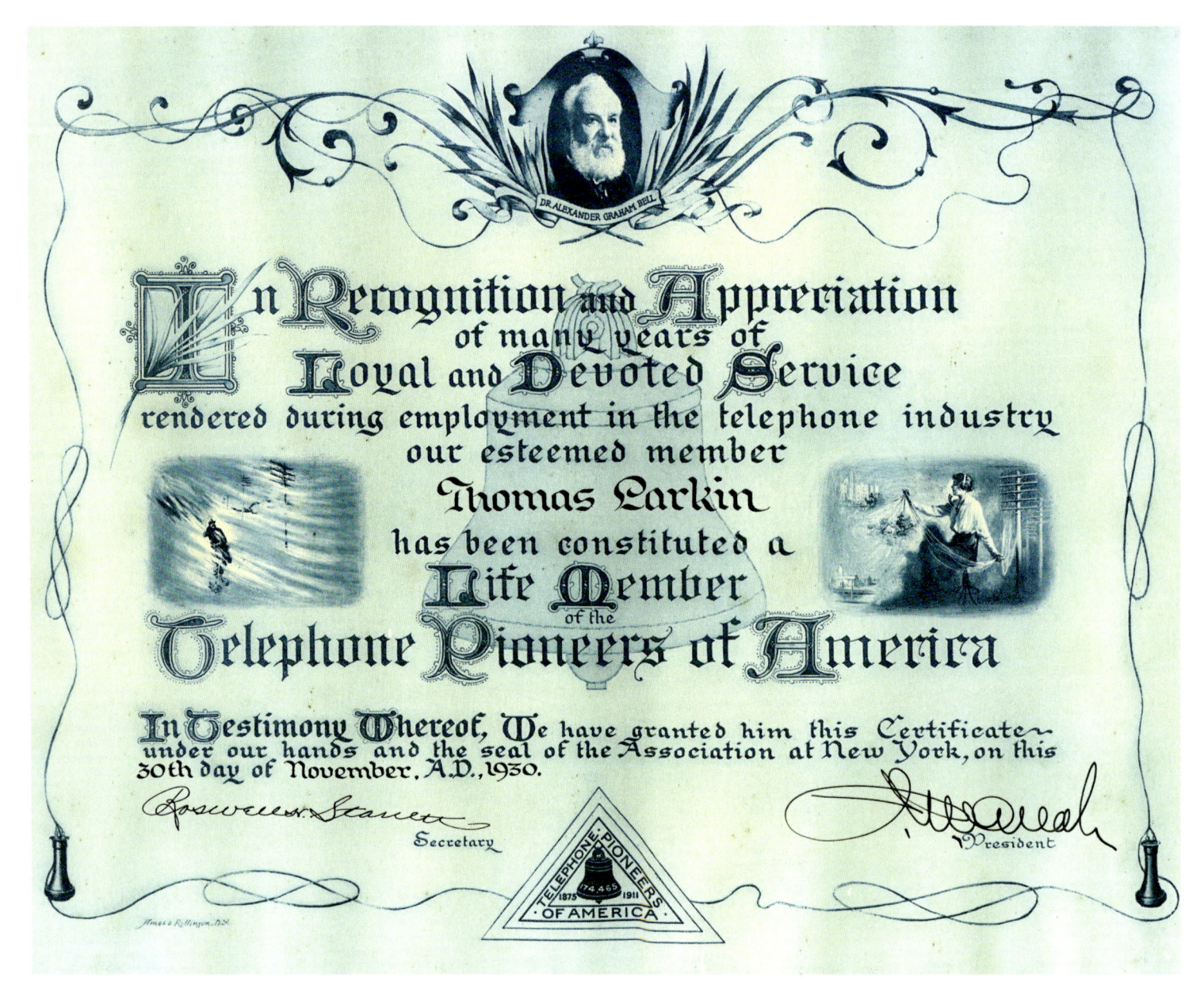

A copy of the original certificate conferring Thomas Larkin with Life Membership of the Telephone Pioneers of America.
Pic.: Michael Larkin.

Chapter 4. *Philadelphia to Pittsburgh*

with the Bell Telephone Company. The impressive original certificate conferring Life Membership of the Telephone Pioneers of America would be something akin to an Honorary Degree by today's standards. The certificate, with the unmistakeable image of Alexander G. Bell and the Telephone Pioneers of America double triangular symbol, is signed by Mr J.S. McCulloh, President, and Mr Roswell H. Starrett, Secretary of the Telephone Company.

He was also presented with an engraved copper cup in recognition of his dedication and service to the telephone industry. This now tarnished and dull cup, was in its day, a gleaming, prestigious award, with its dark blue iconic Bell symbol encircled in an ornate motif.

Thomas's now tattered and worn genuine cowhide leather briefcase, with the imprint on the lock reading, 'Milwaukee Stamping Company', and its tanned interior segments to hold files, notebooks, pencils etc, indicating a supervisory role, is an example of quality American craftsmanship from this era.

On the occasion of his retirement, he was presented with a gold-plated pocket watch, manufactured by the Waltham American Watch Company.

Thomas and Mr Bell met on more than one occasion, and, surprisingly their conversation did not focus on the marvel of the telephone, it focused instead on the similarities between Ireland's Western coastline, the ruggedness of the Scottish Highlands and Bell's adopted homeland of Nova Scotia!

Thomas Larkin's American suitcase has survived the passage of time relatively intact. Note its tanned leather interior compartments. The black, ribbed leather exterior has an imprint on the base reading 'Genuine cowhide leather'. The imprint on the lock reads 'Milwaukee Stamping Company'.
Pic.: Michael Larkin.

Chapter 4. *Philadelphia to Pittsburgh*

PITTSBURGH BACK THEN

When Thomas knocked on that moonlit door of the lodging house on his very first night in Pittsburgh, tired, weary and looking for somewhere to lay his head, the landlady's "welcome to hell" greeting was not what he expected. Very soon he discovered the true meaning of the words. From the Mid 1800s, Pittsburgh was rapidly becoming a gateway to the West. Built on the confluence of the Allegeny, Monongahela and Ohio rivers made the city an ideal location for barges and steam boats to load and unload cargo. The arrival of the railroads brought thousands of people seeking work. However it was the rich deposits of coal, iron ore, lead and zinc that led to the city becoming an industrial heartland.

At one time, Pittsburgh supplied over one third of the United States steel requirements. European, British and Irish immigrants arrived in droves to work in the mills and ancillary industries. One report stated; 'hardened by sweat, heat, poverty and manual labor, it forged its people like the steel that rolled from the mills'. It was common practice for businessmen to remove their 'white' shirt collar by lunchtime as it would have turned black by then. (Men's shirts at the time had detachable collars). It was not unusual for street lights to be lit from mid-day. The 'fog' that Thomas Larkin experienced, on his first days in the city, was in sharp contrast to the fog that sweeps across Clew Bay, enveloping Croagh Patrick and the hills of County Mayo. 'The Smoky City', 'Hell with the lid off' were some of the terms in use at the time to describe

North Side flood district 1911, Lacock Street at Rampart Alley, looking west.
Pic.: Courtesy University of Pittsburgh Library and Archives Centre.

Pittsburgh. Although he didn't understand the 'Welcome to hell' greeting on that first night, he very soon discovered that Pittsburgh was indeed 'one hell of a city'.

The song 'Pittsburgh Town' written by Pete Seeger and performed by Woodie Gutherie, illustrates the city's smoky, smog laden past.

'Pittsburgh town is a smoky 'ol town,

Solid iron from McKeesport down,

Pittsburgh, Lord God, Pittsburgh'

PITTSBURGH TODAY

Fifteen years after Thomas Larkin returned home, David L. Lawrence became Mayor of Pittsburgh in 1946 and later Governor of Pennsylvania. In his inauguration address, he pledged to enhance and clean up his beloved city. He had grown up in a tough, working class Irish neighbourhood, with many run down and abandoned steel mills. He oversaw the implementation of 'Renaissance 1', a plan to revitalise and reinvigorate the city and invite residents and businesses back into the town center. The Pittsburgh Post Gazette stated;

"he loved to tell stories as if he were straight off the boat from County Mayo".

Similar to Bell, Hubbard, Sanders, Vail and others, Lawrence was also a man of vision, with a capacity to embrace individuals and leaders, who would assist him towards the end goals. Thomas was an acquaintance of the Lawrence family and frequently spent time in their company, reminiscing about the 'old days'. What was once the most unliveable city in the U.S.A., Pittsburgh is now the best place to live in the U.S.A. [the Economist 2014], and is described as a city with 'one of the best sky lines in the world'. It is at the cutting edge of technology, innovation, healthcare, financial services and research, and the 'smoky city' of the past has transformed itself into today's majestic, vibrant city. Westport, the town where Thomas Larkin boarded the steam train as he began his emigrant journey, is today the best place to live in Ireland. [Irish Times and Retail Excellence Irl. 2011], and has been the recipient of many National Tidy Towns and other awards.

The Cathedral of Learning forms the centrepiece of the University of Pittsburgh's main campus. This 42-storey, Gothic style structure stands 535ft (163m) tall and is the second tallest university building in the world. Construction commenced in 1926, with the first lecture being delivered in 1931.
Pic.: Michael Larkin.

Chapter 4. *Philadelphia to Pittsburgh*

Aerial view of Pittsburgh, 1930. View of Downtown, facing the Point including parts of the North Side and the Monongahela and Allegheny Wharves. *Pic.: Aerial Photographs of Pittsburgh Collection, University of Pittsburgh*

Chapter 4. *Philadelphia to Pittsburgh*

Pittsburgh - a City of Bridges. A striking view taken from Mt. Washington, (once called Coal Hill, due to its rich coal deposits). The vibrant, attractive Pittsburgh of today contrasts starkly to the city known as 'Hell with the lid off' from the early 1900s. *Pic.: Michael Larkin.*

Chapter 4. *Philadelphia to Pittsburgh*

Photograph of East Carson Street, December 17th, 1921 on Pittsburgh's Southside. Thomas Larkin resided at number 1926 on this street, towards the latter stages of his career. East Carson Street is now designated as one of Pittsburgh's historic districts.

Pic.: Courtesy University of Pittsburgh, Library and Archives Centre

5

MAYOS' WORLD CHAMPIONS OF THE TIME

Thomas Larkin was just ten years old when the Gaelic Athletic Association (G.A.A.) was founded, in Thurles, County Tipperary in 1884.

For him, and his fellow pupils, manual work on their small family farms, in addition to long hours working on the larger estates (if work was available) was commonplace. This allowed little free time, apart from Sundays. After Mass on Sundays, in 'sports fields' around Ballyburke, Killawalla and Ballyheane, neighbouring or townland Gaelic Football teams would compete against each other, not always adhering to the rules of the G.A.A.! Hurling and camogie games were also played. (The O'Duffy Cup, presented annually to the All-Ireland winning camogie team is named in memory of Sean O'Duffy, born in Killawalla 1885).

In the Pittsburgh region, the Allegheny Athletic Association (A.A.A.) Pittsburgh Athletic Association (P.A.A.) and 'another' G.A.A., the Greensburg Athletic Association, were competing against each other in various leagues of American Football. Charlie Atherton, originally a baseball player, born in the same year as Thomas Larkin, is widely credited with 'inventing' the place kick in American football. During weekends, many able-bodied, physically strong, young Irish immigrants would engage in informal Gaelic football or hurling matches. On occasions, American football players, or coaches would attend and observe the levels of skill, in the art of high fielding, place kicking, 'man marking', etc., displayed, by what many deemed to be the 'less cultured' Irish immigrants.

Through the course of his employment, Thomas became an acquaintance of the Rooney Family, who had also emigrated from Ireland. They operated a cafe and saloon, close to Exposition Park, which was home to baseball, American football and even horse racing on occasions. Their eldest son Arthur Joseph excelled in many sports, including baseball, American football and boxing. However, he is best known in later years for his purchase of the semi-professional Pittsburgh football team, which he

Chapter 5. *Mayo's World Champions of the Time*

The former U.S. Ambassador to Ireland, Mr Dan Rooney together with his wife Patricia are photographed receiving a gift of Mayo crystal from Ms. Teresa McHale, Head of Continuing Professional Development (C.P.D.), Hibernia College, on the occasion of the Rooney's visit to County Mayo in November 2009.
Pic.: Michael Donnelly, Mayo Pix.

Walking the fields and muddy pathway to Ballyburke National School, helping out on the small farm, or working on the larger estates, allowed little time for engaging in sport of any kind. However, Thomas did play some Gaelic football, and participated in track and field events in the surrounding area. Locals and some of his peers deemed him to have been good at the 'long jump' and 'a great runner'.

In the same year that he arrived in Philadelphia, a young Mayo man named Martin Sheridan, arrived in New York who would go on to become what was reported later 'the greatest track and field athlete of all time'.

The bronze bust of Martin Sheridan, located in his native Bohola. The memorial was unveiled in May 1966, by Gene Tunney Jnr, son of World Champion boxer Gene Tunney. *Pic.: Michael Larkin.*

re-named the Pittsburgh Steelers. Following his death in August 1988, his eldest son, Dan, became the owner and Chairman of the team. Dan married Patricia Regan, her family having emigrated from County Mayo in the early 1900s. He was the co-founder of the American Ireland Fund, alongside Anthony O'Reilly, former Irish rugby international and C.E.O. of the H.J. Heinz Corporation. Dan Rooney served as U.S. Ambassador to Ireland from 2009 to 2012. He died peacefully at his home in Pittsburgh on April 13th 2017.

Martin Sheridan

Martin Sheridan was born in the village of Bohola, just over 15 miles (25km) from Thomas Larkin's home, on March 28th 1881. He emigrated to New York, joined the New York Police Force, went on to win nine Olympic medals and numerous other awards and trophies, representing the U.S.A. between 1901 and 1911. Thomas had the privilege of witnessing some of Sheridan's achievements, and joined with hundreds of fellow Irish immigrants in attending the 1904 Olympic Games in St. Louis to cheer on their Mayo-born hero.

Gene 'the fighting marine' Tunney

Very close to Martin Sheridan's birthplace, another family also emigrated to New York. Gene 'the fighting marine' Tunney was born in New York on May 25th 1897, his parents having earlier emigrated from Kiltimagh. He was only once defeated in his heavyweight boxing career by Harry Grebb, Pittsburgh. Tunney's wife, Mary 'Poly' Lauder, was a niece of Ironworks founder, Andrew Carnegie, and they both visited Pittsburgh regularly.

Gentleman Jim James Corbett

James Corbett, (Gentleman Jim) was born in Los Angeles, on September 1st, 1866. His parents had emigrated from Ballinrobe, County Mayo. In a boxing career spanning 17 years (1886 - 1903) he won his first World Heavyweight Title in New Orleans, in 1892. He visited his ancestral homeland as world champion in 1894, and gave a boxing

Gene Tunney, heavyweight champion boxer
Pic.: Courtesy Harris & Ewing collection, Library of Congress.

exhibition in Ballinrobe Town Hall. He gave the proceeds of the event to his uncle, Fr. James Corbett, who was Parish Priest in Partry. In 1924, he engaged in a 'friendly' boxing match with the upcoming future World Champion, Gene Tunney, in New York. Jim Corbett's brother, Joe was an accomplished baseball player.

The impressive stained glass window in St. Mary's Church, Partry, donated by James J. Corbett following his visit to his ancestral homeland in 1894. *Pic.: Michael Larkin.*

Johnny Kilbane

Thomas Larkin joined the estimated crowd of 100,000 people on St. Patrick's Day 1912 in Cleveland, to welcome home World Featherweight Champion, Johnny Kilbane. Kilbane retained the title from 1912 until 1923, the longest unbroken period in the division's history. He was born on April 9th, 1889, in Cleveland. His parents had emigrated from Achill many years earlier. Thomas Larkin, along with most other Irish Americans, were very proud of their sporting heroes. He recounted in later years having met many of the above sporting men and witnessing some of their sporting achievements.

THE PENNSYLVANIA CUP

Thomas Larkin had long since departed from this life when in 2016 the Pennsylvania Cup was presented to the Caithaoireach (Mayor) of Mayo County Council, Councillor Al McDonnell, who accepted it on behalf of the people of Mayo at home and abroad. This magnificent cup was originally presented to Mick Mulderrig, Captain of the Mayo Senior Football team, on the occasion of their visit to the east coast of the U.S.A. in 1932. Thousands flocked to meet and greet the team as they arrived for exhibition games in New York, Boston, Rhode Island and New Jersey.

Influential New York based Attorney, Mayo man William (Bill) O Dwyer, who would later become the 100th Mayor of New York, invested heavily in ensuring the trip would be successful. Former World Heavyweight Boxing Champion, Gentleman Jim Corbett 'threw in' the ball at the

Councillor Al McDonnell, Cathaoirleach (Chairman) of Mayo County Council accepts the Pennsylvania Cup from Mr Pat McNicholas, Cricklewood, London, who had this prestigious cup in his possession for a number of years through his friendship with members of the Mulderrig family. L. - R. John Condon, Director of Services, Castlebar Municipal District, Mayo County Council, Cllr. Henry Kenny, Cllr. Al McDonnell, Pat McNicholas and Michael Larkin. *Pic.: Michael Donnelly, Mayo Pix.*

Polo Grounds, for the New York versus Mayo game. However, it was in Philadelphia, where they played two games against a Pennsylvania selection, that captured most headlines. Following their success, they were deemed 'World Gaelic Football Champions', when the Captain was presented with the Cup, amid scenes of great joy and jubilation. Most of this team formed the nucleus of Mayo's first All-Ireland winning team of 1936. In the intervening years, the Pennsylvania Cup was deemed to have been lost through the passage of time. However, in September 2016, a very special and historic ceremony was held in the chamber of Mayo County Council, where this magnificent cup was presented to the Cathaoirleach of Mayo County Council, on behalf of the people of County Mayo at home and abroad.

Chapter 5. *Mayo's World Champions of the Time*

The Mayo Football team which travelled to America in 1932, and were presented with the 'Pennsylvania Cup'.
Back, Left - Right: Purty Kelly, Jim O'Dwyer, Sean Moran, Mick Moran, Seamus O'Malley, Jim Forde, Patsy Flannelly.
Center: John Egan, Sean Lavin, Paddy Quinn, John Clarke, Bernie Durcan, Paddy Moclair, Dick Hearns, Tom Bourke.
Front: Phil Hoban, Jack Kenny, John Culkin, Gerard Courell, Mick Mulderrig (Captain), Paddy Munnelly, Tom Feeney, Jimmy Curran.
Pic.: Courtesy Henry Kenny.

6

THE TELEPHONE PIONEERS OF AMERICA

In an American context the term 'Pioneer' is frequently associated with images of settlers who journeyed to the American Mid West in convoys of wagons or on horseback, in search of adventure, prospecting for gold, or simply to acquire more land. A.G. Bell, Watson, Sanders, Hubbard, Vail and others were also pioneers in terms of inventing and investing in the telephone.

However, without teams of linemen, telephone operators, installers, fixers and many others, Bell's dream of the human voice travelling across wires, over long distances, would not have come to fruition.

The Bell Company, later to become the American Telephone and Telegraph Company (AT&T), was expanding rapidly throughout North America. While Bell and his associates were men of vision and wisdom, they were also anxious to provide more than just a great telephone network. In 1910 Henry Pope and a number of other senior employees suggested that the industry's success warranted a 'giving back' to communities, towns and cities through involvement in education, life enrichment, environmental and other projects to assist the underprivileged and marginalised. Theodore N. Vail, then President of AT&T, concurred, resulting in the first meeting to further those goals. This first meeting, which led to the formation of the Telephone Pioneers of America, was held

The specially commissioned Pioneers crest unveiled as part of the Pioneers Centenary celebrations, Boston, November 2011.
Image: courtesy G. McLaughlin, Fort Pitt Pioneers.

Chapter 6. The Telephone Pioneers of America

in the Somerset Hotel, Boston, on November 2nd, 1911. A. G. Bell received membership card number one. The aim of the new organisation was to 'preserve the legacy of the original pioneers through a spirit of volunteering and giving back to one's community'. Today the Telephone Pioneers of America, or Pioneers, as they are referred to in more recent times, are the world's largest, industry specific group of employees and retirees, dedicated to 'answering the call' of communities in need and assisting with environmental and educational projects throughout North America. Since their establishment in 1911, the Pioneers have celebrated landmark anniversaries with many special events. In the same year as County Mayo won its first All-Ireland Football Final, the Pioneers Silver Jubilee in 1936 was celebrated simultaneously across the U.S.A. and Canada. In 1986 Minneapolis hosted the 75th anniversary Pioneer celebrations incorporating the theme of '75 years of giving back - just the beginning' with U.S President Ronald Regan addressing the gathering.

On November 2nd, 2011, Boston Mayor Tom Menino welcomed over 1,200 Pioneers to the city where the Pioneers were founded 100 years beforehand.

One of the greatest natural disasters to hit the U.S.A. in recent times was the powerful Hurricane Katrina, on August 29th, 2005. Pioneers from throughout the entire continent of North America answered the call and played a major role in the mammoth humanitarian efforts following the hurricane. Fr. Michael Tracey, Killawalla, grand-nephew of Thomas Larkin, saw his parish in Bay St.

The 'Angel of Light' statue, dedicated to the thousands of volunteers who helped in the recovery in the aftermath of Hurricane Kathrina, stands in front of Our Lady of the Gulf Catholic Church in Bay St. Louis, Mississippi.
Pic.: Courtesy Fr. Michael Treacy.

Louis, Mississippi, virtually disappear, resulting in hundreds of casualties, and hundreds more becoming homeless. His book 'She Was No Lady' tells of the hurricane and life at that time. How ironic, that only three years before the Pioneers Centennial, Fr. Michael Tracey would be invited to this same City of Boston where the Pioneers were founded, to be acknowledged as the Boston-Mayo Person of the Year 2008, in recognition of his outstanding work in the aftermath of Hurricane Katrina.

In his acceptance speech Fr Tracey stated;

"This is one of the proudest days of my life, since my ordination, and is indeed very humbling. I didn't do anything dramatic, anything special. I did something everyone here would do if they were in my shoes. The cards that are dealt to us in life, we play. They are not of our choosing, it is up to us to play them as best we can".

Thomas Larkin would have been very proud indeed, to have witnessed his grand-nephew Fr Tracey being acknowledged for simply 'answering the call', just as he had done many times, as a Telephone Pioneer of America.

Today, the Pioneer Headquarters are located in Denver, Colorado. Their symbol, a double triangle encompassing the words 'Telephone Pioneers of America', incorporates the Bell symbol in the center. The number 174,465 is the U.S patent number issued to Bell for the invention of the speaking telegraph. The three sides of the triangle symbolize FELLOWSHIP, LOYALTY AND SERVICE. Since their establishment in 1911 the Pioneers have enriched the lives of many, helped regenerate numerous communities, and continue to uphold that proud legacy of the original Telephone Pioneers.

THE TELEPHONE PIONEERS OF AMERICA PAY A SPECIAL TRIBUTE

In October 2016, the President of the Fort Pitt Pioneer Chapter, Pittsburgh, Ms. Gerry McLaughlin, made a significant and very special visit to County Mayo, where she placed a bell-shaped wreath along with three white carnations, symbolising Fellowship, Loyalty and Service at the headstone of Thomas Larkin in Killawalla cemetery.

As a light Atlantic mist drifted across the nearby Partry Mountains and the leaves gently fluttered on the trees in the late Autumn breeze, this poignant and simple wreath laying ceremony symbolized a transatlantic link much deeper and stronger than any cable or digital connection. In what was an emotional and moving tribute Ms. McLaughlin stated;

Telephone Pioneers of America triangular symbol.
Image: courtesy G. McLaughlin, Fort Pitt Pioneers.

Chapter 6. The Telephone Pioneers of America

"We, Gerry and John McLaughlin, representing the New Vision Pioneers from the United States of America, have come together in County Mayo, Ireland, with members of the Larkin Family and their friends, to remember our esteemed Life Member, Thomas Larkin. We recognise and honor the many years of loyal and devoted service he rendered to the Telephone Pioneers of America during his many years of employment in the telephone industry. We are thankful to God for Thomas Larkin's life and his efforts in fulfilling the Pioneer mission. Even after he retired from the Bell Telephone Company, in Pittsburgh PA, and returned home to Ireland, he continued to foster the pioneering spirit by charitable activities throughout his life. As we go forward with our daily lives, let us keep his memory in our hearts. May we so honor Thomas Larkin."

October 8th, 2016.

The President, Ms. McLaughlin, also spent some time on the Larkin farm in Derrew, stood on the same ground and walked on some of the winding laneways and pathways, once trodden by Thomas Larkin.

Later the President and her husband, John were overwhelmed to be welcomed by An Taoiseach, Mr Enda Kenny, T.D., Senators and elected members of Mayo County Council to the Linenhall Arts Centre, Castlebar, where Thomas Larkin's contribution as a Telephone Pioneer of America was duly recognised.

Ms. Gerry McLaughlin, with Shane, Michael and Micheál Larkin at the headstone of Thomas Larkin in Killawalla cemetery.
Pic.: Courtesy Tom and Mary Tracey.

Caitriona Doyle, John and Gerry McLaughlin, Michael Larkin, Councillors Martin McLoughlin and Thérèse Ruane, Senator Marie Louise O'Donnell, pictured in the Linenhall Arts Centre.
Pic.: Courtesy Alison Laredo.

7

THE HOMECOMING

Coming close to his retirement, Thomas Larkin had a little more time to reflect on his life's journey to date. He had travelled many highways and enjoyed a distinguished career with the Bell Telephone Company. However, more and more he was silently wondering to himself, 'Is there anybody there?' This time he wasn't wondering if there was anybody in the lodging house that he first set foot in following his arrival in Pittsburgh. He was wondering instead if there was anybody remaining in the old Larkin homestead back in County Mayo. The powerful and evocative song 'Paddy', written and preformed by singer/songwriter Gerry Carney, gives us some insight into the reasons why many Irish emigrants lost touch with their homeland.

You can never explain just what happened,
The years seem to pass like a day,
Sometimes he thinks of the boreen,
That led to his home from the lane,
And the fields that he worked with his father,
He'll never see them again.

Most Irish emigrants resented being forced to leave their native homeland. They also carried with them a deep hatred of landlordism. Many vowed never to set foot in Ireland again. Families were frequently divided over who should inherit the small farm. Working long hours in coal mines, steel mills or construction sites, meant that writing a letter home became a chore. Frequent changes of address or relocation to where work was more plentiful meant that many letters from 'home' never reached the emigrant son or daughter. Then, as the words from the song 'Paddy' describe 'the years seemed to pass like a day', meant that far too much time had elapsed since the last letter or greeting card had been written. Now it was too late.

Despite many years having passed since Thomas either received or sent a letter home, Ireland was always on his mind. It was now coming close to the end of his career, and having achieved much more than he ever thought possible, he pondered quietly about Ireland.

Chapter 7. The Homecoming

Mary and Bridget Burke, photographed in Boston 1911.
Pic.: Courtesy Kelly / Walsh family Boston.

From Larkin's Way to Larkin's Field

Little did Michael Larkin realise, as he worked on his small farm back in Derrew, that in faraway Pittsburgh, his brother Thomas Larkin had walked almost every morning and evening along the street 'Larkin's Way' on Pittsburgh's South Side. Neither did Thomas Larkin realise, that across the Atlantic Ocean, back in Derrew, on the south side of Castlebar, the landlord's grip had long since been loosened on the lands of Ireland, and his brother Michael Larkin was now tilling the small Larkin family farm. Similar to the all too familiar story of Irish emigration, or in the words from the song 'Paddy' referred to earlier, in Thomas Larkin's case, far too many years had elapsed since the last handwritten letter had been sent or received. However, either through fate or good fortune, contact would soon be established once more.

Michael, who never emigrated, married Mary Burke in February 1915 and they resided in the 'new' bungalow, built in 1911 to replace the old thatched cottage in Derrew.

Mary Burke, born in 1886, had also spent some time in the U.S.A. She emigrated to Boston in 1907, later sending home the £7.12 shillings ($40 approx) fare, inviting her younger sister Bridget to join her. Bridget didn't need a second invitation, she joined with her sister in Boston, and later married Andrew Kelly, who had arrived in the U.S.A. from County Galway some time earlier. Mary returned home in 1914 and married Michael Larkin the following year in St Patrick's Church, Killawalla.

Chapter 7. *The Homecoming*

Thomas Larkin, throughout his career, had helped to connect many families and businesses via the telephone - now he was expanding his own network and hoping to connect with his homeland. With more time to spare, he spent some time travelling throughout the United States. One of his journeys brought him east once again to Philadelphia. This was his first time returning to the city since he first arrived there in 1899. The Philadelphia Mayo Association was established in 1905 with the aim of maintaining connectivity between the Mayo diaspora in East Pennsylvania, and their native county in Ireland. Thomas attended one of their events, and during the course of conversation he was given the address of a Michael Murphy, originally from Ballyburke. The following day with the handwritten address on a piece of notepaper, he attempted to locate Murphy's whereabouts. Both men would have known each other from attending Ballyburke National School. Carefully following the directions he was given the previous evening, he eventually arrived at the address. As the door slowly opened, he asked "Is there a Michael Murphy living at this address?". "Yes", replied the lady - "but he moved on from here over six months ago". The initial "Yes" sounded good - however "moving on over six months ago" in a city the size of Philadelphia dimmed Thomas' excitement somewhat. However, the lady did have details of where Murphy may have moved onto. The following day, Thomas was relaxing in a saloon, a Saturday around lunchtime, when a number of men from a nearby construction site entered ... and there he was!. Michael Murphy was amongst the group of men who were finishing work for that week. Despite not having met for almost a full lifetime, both men instantly recognised each other. Inside the space of one hour, both men, despite being over 3,000 miles from home, had 'walked' the laneways, 'ploughed' the fields and 'saved the hay', as they talked about bygone days. However, Thomas had one burning question to ask; "Tell me, are there any of the Larkin's alive back in Derrew?" Michael Murphy pondered for a moment: "Yes there are" he replied. His next statement was even more exciting; "I'm going over there next week to help my father on the farm". Instantly Thomas said to Michael "If I write a letter will you deliver it to Derrew?". Murphy was only too delighted to oblige. Inside the space of fifteen minutes Thomas had the letter written on the piece of notepaper he procured from the barman. He handed the tightly sealed envelope to Michael and stated, "You can tell them I may go back home someday". With that both men went their separate ways. Weeks passed, Thomas continued to receive mail through his letterbox, but no overseas mail. However, after about eight weeks, the long awaited letter, bearing the Irish postmark and stamp with the shamrock and Celtic design insignia arrived. This was the handwritten letter from home, with the address on the top right hand corner reading 'Derrew, Ballyheane, Castlebar, County Mayo',

Pic. Michael Walsh - from 'The History of Killawalla Post Office / Killawalla at Home & Away 2011.

61

and commencing with the words "Dear Thomas. We're delighted to hear you are alive and well … It finished with the invitation "perhaps you might come home sometime to see us". This was the first time Thomas had seen the words, 'Derrew, Ballyheane …" since he first arrived in the U.S.A. Almost immediately, he started to pen another letter to County Mayo. Depending on weather conditions, mail crossing the Atlantic at the time could take up to 15 days to reach its destination. Significant amounts of mail was carried in both directions, with much of the mail from the U.S.A. having dollar remittances enclosed with the handwritten letter. Two or three further letters were exchanged between Pittsburgh and County Mayo over the course of the next few months. Thomas' final letter from Pittsburgh stated 'by the time you receive this letter I will be half way across the Atlantic'. Following a lifetime in America the long lost 'stranger' was returning home!

THE HOMECOMING

As the ship steamed eastwards across the Atlantic, Thomas was looking forward to firstly stepping on Irish soil at Queenstown, and then, making that long awaited journey back to Mayo. His impending arrival home in August 1931, after such a long absence generated much local interest.

Today, we are accustomed to precise and accurate timetables for aircraft, rail and coach services. In the era of steam travel, there were frequent breakdowns, services were unreliable, and times of arrival at destinations could only be estimated.

The song, 'Are ya right there Michael', composed by Percy French (1902) illustrates the unreliability of steam train travel at the time.

You run for the train in the mornin',

The excursion train's startin' at eight,

It's there for an hour you will wait,

And as you're waitin' on the train,

You'll hear the guard sing this refrain,

Are ya right there Michael, are ya right?

Do you think that we'll be there before the night?,

Well I couldn't say for sure,

But we might now, Michael, so we might"

Michael and Mary Larkin spared no effort in ensuring that the house, farmyard and sheds looked neat and tidy. Sheds were whitewashed, doors and windows painted, broken down stone walls rebuilt, even the chimney was cleared to ensure the open fire burned brightly. Finally that day arrived. On Thursday, August 27th, 1931 the 3.30pm steam train screeched to a halt, 'only' one hour behind schedule at Castlebar rail station.

Through the crowded platform, Michael Larkin and members of his young family were eagerly looking from left to right. His daughter Mary Kate suddenly exclaimed, "Dad, is that him?" Sure enough this was Thomas Larkin, back home once again in Mayo.

Now it was time for the journey to his home village. The shrill sound of the steam train whistle blew as the train continued on its journey towards Westport. "Shall I call a cab?" Thomas asked. "No need to", Michael replied, "I've got the horse and cart over there". This was Ireland, not Pittsburgh after all!

The village of Ballyheane is approximately five miles (eight kms) south of Castlebar, on the N84 roadway, leading to Ballinrobe and onwards to Galway. The sound of the Clydesdale's iron shod hooves on the N84's stone surface was sweet music as they galloped along towards Ballyheane. St Mary's National School, built in 1887 was a relatively new building when Thomas emigrated, now it was almost 50 years old.

Pic.: Michael Larkin

Onwards through the village, the cemetery on the left, the Royal Irish Constabulary (R.I.C.) Barracks on the right, the fairgreen, blacksmith's forge, three licensed premises, St. Patrick's Church, the Post Office and the Church of Ireland with its tall spire. Turning right onto the L1817 minor road, the townlands of Cloonaghmore and Killadeer on the right, Derrew to the left, the spring well by the roadside and eventually the laneway to LARKINS! - Home at Last! This would be his first time entering the 'new' bungalow, built in 1911 on the site of the old thatched cottage where he was born in 1874.

In the weeks and months that followed, neighbours and friends gathered around the fireside to meet and greet Thomas, and especially to hear his descriptions of lifestyles, work opportunities and the sheer scale and size of the America he had just left behind. His knowledge and description of telephones, radio and electricity fascinated young and old alike. He was invited to speak in local national schools, including his old school in Ballyburke.

He also met with elected members of Mayo County Council and personnel from the Department of Posts and Telegraphs, where he outlined his vision of how telecommunication would evolve in Ireland in the years ahead. Senator John E. McEllin and other business men held a number of meetings throughout Mayo with a view to establishing an industry in the region. At one of the meetings, Thomas outlined his familiarity with the Bollman Hat Company, established in Pennsylvania in 1868. This company had a high reputation throughout the U.S.A. for the production and top quality head gear. While the Bollman Hat Company had no involvement, Thomas was proud to be in attendance when the first sod was turned for the establishment of a new hat factory in Castlebar in May 1939.

Chapter 7. *The Homecoming*

1930s - Agriculture in Ireland and the U.S.A.

In 1930s Ireland, when Thomas Larkin decided to return home, the economy was almost totally dependent on agriculture and ancillary industries, such as bacon curing, textiles, sugar processing, flour milling, etc. In County Mayo, the average farm size was less than 20 acres (8ha), with household incomes supplemented by sterling and dollar remittances from sons and daughters who had emigrated.

Thomas always retained his interest in activities related to nature and the soil. In the U.S.A. he took a keen interest in the use of horse and diesel powered machinery used on the vast farms in the Pennsylvania / Ohio regions.

While Henry Ford established his first production plant outside the U.S.A. in Cork in 1917 to manufacture Fordson Tractors, most were destined for the export market as the meagre income from the small farms did not justify the purchase of an 'Iron Horse'. Despite the small farms and field sizes, most farms at the time grew crops of barley, oats and rye in addition to potato and vegetables. The first combine harvester was patented in the U.S.A. in 1835. Many variants followed, initially powered by teams of working horses, later by steam and later again by diesel. In 1911 the Holt Manufacturing Company, California, later to become known as today's Giant Caterpillar Company, produced a self-propelled harvester. The Reaper and Binder, which tied the sheaves of grain with twine, was also in widespread use in the American Midwest. Famous names associated with the manufacture of agricultural

Scale model replica of an early Fordson Tractor.
Pic.: Michael Larkin

machinery in the U.S.A, such as McCormick, Deering (later to amalgamate and form International Harvester (I.H.), John Deere, Allis Chalmers, Massey Harris and others, continued to produce larger, more modern machines for use on American farms. Similar to his conversations regarding the telephone, when Thomas outlined how 'giant machines, capable of harvesting over 40 acres per day and pulled by teams of up to twenty horses', were in use on large farms in the U.S.A., listeners gasped in awe. At a time in rural County Mayo where the ridges of the failed potato crop from the famine era were still visible, few could comprehend the vastness and scale of the great American plains. Many of the small farms did not own even one working horse. Thomas' description of giant harvesters being pulled by twenty horses could not be visualised in the impoverished rural Ireland at the time.

Chapter 7. *The Homecoming*

It's ironic that almost one hundred years later, Thomas Larkin's great-grand-nephew, Micheál Larkin spent a semester as part of his Agricultural Degree studies on one of the modern combine harvesters in America's Midwestern Grain Belt. His other great-grand-nephew, Shane Larkin, also undertook a U.S.A. work experience programme in Boston – that same city where A.G. Bell invented the telephone in 1876.

An unassuming private man, in the true spirit of his Telephone Pioneer friends he had left behind in the U.S., Thomas 'answered the call' in his local neighbourhood and was a silent benefactor to many not-for-profit community and Church organisations.

While the U.S.A. was slowly recovering from the Great Depression of 1929, Ireland's Economic Trade War with Britain was only beginning. The Great Depression had impacted on the lives of thousands of Americans, nevertheless, their standard of living was superior to life in Ireland at the time. In Ireland, poor road networks, unreliable public transport, lack of electricity and telephones and hard, manual labour on the small farms, meant little had changed from the time he first emigrated.

Micheál and Shane Larkin, great grand nephews of Thomas Larkin, undertook work placement programmes in the U.S.A.
Pics.: Michael Larkin

Convoy of large Kenworth trucks transporting corn-harvesting machinery in Kansas *Pic.: courtesy American Harvest Trail / Micheál Larkin*

Chapter 7. *The Homecoming*

Throughout 1931, his first year at home, he seriously contemplated returning once again to the U.S.A. However, he immersed himself in everyday life on the farm and played an active role in saving the hay, corn harvesting, stonewall building and other farm chores.

Today, some of the dry stone walls, many incorporating stiles and steps that he painstakingly built, are still visible around the farm. He participated in a 'meitheal' (gathering) each Autumn, whereby ten or more neighbours assisted each other on a rota system in the harvesting of corn, threshing or digging potatoes. Most Saturdays he would take some time out to visit one of the local towns. On his return home by late afternoon he would usually be greeted by his young nieces and nephews in the village of Ballyheane. Here he would hand out some candy and chocolates and say "run along now, have the kettle boiled by the time I get home". By the time he would have walked the short distance from the village to the farm house, the black cast iron kettle, suspended by a hook from the crane, over a blazing open turf fire, would be singing and hissing. The delph teapot, sitting on a wrought iron tripod, would be full of freshly brewed tea. All would sit around the large oak table with its colourful oil-cloth covering and enjoy tea from the blue and white willow patterned cups, homemade brown soda bread plus 'goodies' and 'surprises' Thomas had purchased earlier that day.

Each Sunday morning, regardless of weather, he would walk the two mile distance to attend 10a.m. mass in St. Patrick's Church, Killawalla, his local parish church. At a

The willow patterned plate and milk jug - the only remaining pieces of crockery from the old Larkin homestead.
Pic.: Michael Larkin

St Patrick's Church, Killawalla
Pic.: Michael Larkin

Chapter 7. *The Homecoming*

time when Saturday evening masses were unheard of, there was a very high attendance at Sunday morning Church services throughout Ireland. Following the Mass celebrated in Latin at the time, men and women would gather around the chapel doorway and discuss local happenings, events, forthcoming marriages or recent deaths. Meanwhile, the Bell Telephone Company remained in regular contact and kept him updated on developments in telecommunications throughout the U.S.A.

TOWNLAND OF DERREW

Derrew is situated in the Parish of Ballintubber, Barony of Carra, one of the nine Baronies in County Mayo, represented by the nine yew trees on the County Mayo Crest.

The majestic, triangular image of Croagh Patrick, looking west from the Larkin farm in Derrew.
Pic.: Michael Larkin

The name Derrew is an anglicised version of Doire, or An Díthreabh, meaning 'a wilderness of oak trees'. In the distant past, large tracts of Ireland was covered by forestry, much of it being native Irish oak. County Derry (Condae Doire) with the same spelling as Derrew in Irish, is known as the 'Oak Leaf County'. Mayo, when translated from its Irish name Maigh Eo, means 'The Plain of the Yew Trees'. Hence the significance of the nine yew trees bordering the crest, representing each Barony in the County.

The crosses represent the Catholic Dioceses of the county, with the ship illustrating Mayo's maritime history.

Mayo Crest
Pic.: Mayo County Council

Chapter 7. *The Homecoming*

According to the 1895 Ordnance Survey of Ireland, the total area of Derrew comprises 329 acres, 3 roods and 4 perches (137.44ha). However, Derrew is divided into Derrew (old) and Derrew. Derrew (old) comprises 139 acres 3 roods and 19 perches (80.84ha). In many ways the townland of Derrew (old) had not changed significantly since Thomas emigrated. While the old thatched cottages had been replaced by new bungalows, the same four family names of Higgins, Heneghan and both Larkins were still there. The majestic, triangular image of Croagh Patrick to the west was exactly as he would have remembered.

The river that formed part of the boundary between Derrew and Killawullaun continued to flow southwards to join the Aille river. The Aille river flowing from the Partry mountains is one of Ireland's longest underground rivers. Pollatoomary cave is situated where the river re-emerges in Ballyburke, having travelled underground for a distance of more than 2.5 miles (4km). In July 2008, a Polish cave diver, Arthur Kozlawski set a new British and Irish record when he reached a depth of 103m (338ft.) in this cave. [*Explorer plunges to new depths.* Emer Gallagher, Mayo News, July 16th, 2008.]

However, when Thomas gazed eastwards, there were major changes since the time of his emigration. What had been a vast tract of uninhabited land was now home to five new families, who had been transferred from the townland of Cullintra to Derrew as part of the Congested Districts Board (C.D.B) land re-structuring programme.

Following the Land War (1879-1882), a number of Acts

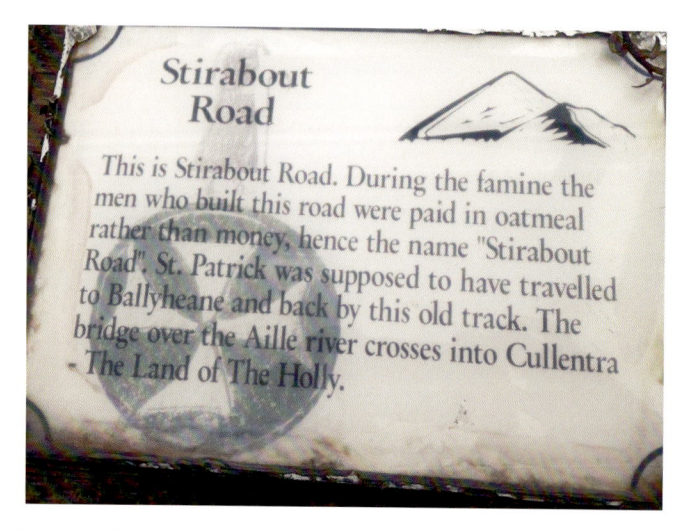

The wording on this sign situated close to the ancient Tóchar Phádraig (St. Patrick's pathway), graphically illustrates the harsh reality of the potato famine in this region, when workers were paid with oatmeal during the building of this roadway.
Pic.: Michael Larkin

were passed in the British Parliament, hoping to appease Irish tenant farmers. Michael Davitt, co-founder of the Irish National Land League, demanded an end to landlordism, so as to allow the tenant farmers regain outright ownership of the lands they worked on. The Land League's slogan was 'The land of Ireland for the people of Ireland'. Progress remained slow throughout the 1800s. Gladstone's Act established the Irish Land Commission (I.L.C.). Other Acts followed including the Ashbourne Act (1885), Balfour Act (1891), which established the Congested District Board. However, it was the Wyndham Land Purchase Act (1903), which heralded the demise of landlordism. This Act facilitated the transfer of over 9,000,000 acres of land from absentee landlords, into the hands of small tenant farmers. The movement of the five families, from the very congested townland of Cullintra, to lands in Derrew, formerly in the ownership of Sir Robert Lynch Blosse, meant a new lease of life for the families concerned. A 'new' roadway was constructed along the route of a much older pathway. The southern end of this pathway was known as 'Stirabout Road', as the labourers were paid with ration tickets which were redeemable for oatmeal or corn during the potato famine. Today all of the Congested District Board bungalows have been modernised. While some family names have changed over time, many of the farms have enlarged further, with cattle and sheep rearing being the predominant type of farming activity today. Up to the 1970s all of the farms were self sufficient, with poultry, pigs, sheep, cattle and an abundance of vegetables for domestic use, or for sale in local towns. All households had access to bogland, where peat, or turf was harvested for use in the large open fireplace.

While emigration continued, much of it was in the form of migration to Britain for periods of nine months to work on construction sites or on some of the larger farms. Today off-farm employment or other forms of self-employment generates the main source of household income.

Up until the time of his death on March 4th, 1953, Thomas Larkin led an active lifestyle and enjoyed good health throughout his retirement years. He is buried in the Larkin family plot in Killawalla cemetery.

A neatly built turf stack on the roadside in Killawullaun bogland.
Pic. Michael Larkin

The final resting place of Thomas Larkin in Killawalla Cemetery.
Pic. Michael Larkin

Chapter 7. The Homecoming

Connaught Telegraph, March 4th, 1953

OBITUARY

MR. THOMAS LARKIN, DERREW, BALLYHEANE

It is with feelings of deepest sorrow and regret we announce the death of Mr. Thomas Larkin, Derrew, Ballyheane, which sad event occurred after a prolonged illness at the residence of his nephew, Mr. John Larkin. The news of his passing came as a profound shock, not only to his bereaved relatives, but to the whole neighbourhood, where he was noted for his Christian charity and generosity. A devout and fervent Catholic, he was a life-long member of the Sacred Heart Sodality and was loved by all who had the pleasure of knowing him. He emigrated to America at an early age and was employed by the Bell Telephone Co. of Pittsburgh, Pennsylvania, from which post he retired on pension in 1932, and being endowed with a love of the land of his birth, he returned to his birthplace to take the rest he so deservedly earned. It was a testimony to the respect and trust in which he was held by the Bell Telephone Co. that Mr. Ingans, the director of the company, was a regular correspondent of the deceased up to the time of his death. The remains were removed to Killawalla Church at 4.30pm on Thursday evening, and the large concourse of sympathisers present marked the high esteem in which the deceased was held. The interment took place in Killawalla Cemetery after 9.30am Mass. Rev. Fr. Jennings officiated at the grave-side. To his bereaved relatives our sincere sympathy is extended in their great sorrow.

8

MY JOURNEY

The slogan 'nothing beats being there' is adopted by the Gaelic Athletic Association (G.A.A.), in an effort to entice supporters and members of the public, to attend live G.A.A. fixtures. That incredible atmosphere, the roar of the crowd, the build up to a major game, discussions on team selection, raised expectations, pre and post game analysis - nothing beats being there!

In a similar way, I was determined to 'go there' - to Pittsburgh and beyond, in an attempt to 'walk' in the footsteps of this Telephone Pioneer, to discover at least some aspects of his journey, carry out some research and visualise the Pittsburgh region as it was in the early 1900s. I had also been privileged to receive an invitation from the Chief Executive of the Ireland - U.S. Council, Mr Roddy Feeley, to exhibit some of Thomas Larkin's memorabilia at one of their prestigious events in Dublin. Here, the United States Ambassador to Ireland, Mr Kevin O'Malley and Mr Greg Varisco, Chief Operations Officer of Aqua Comms, addressed the invited guests on the theme 'Ireland / U.S.A.

Former United States Ambassador to Ireland, Kevin O'Malley (left), with Mr Greg Varisco, CEO Aqua Comms and Michael Larkin.
Pic.: courtesy Lensmen Photography.

Connectivity - Past, Present and Future'. Mr Varisco outlined in great detail the methodology and technology used in the installation of the 3,400 mile (5,500km) transatlantic fiber optic cable connecting the East coast of the U.S.A. with County Mayo. In referring to County Mayo, Mr Varisco stated:

Chapter 8. My Journey

"How ironic it is that right now the most modern fiber optic cable of its type in the world will reach landfall in Killala, County Mayo. Over 100 years ago, Thomas Larkin from County Mayo delivered telephone connectivity into the American Mid-West, which was at the time equally as modern as today's fiber optic technology. It is indeed fitting that County Mayo, birthplace of a telephone pioneer of America, is the landing point for today's ultra-modern transatlantic cable".

Mr Jim Lamb, Honorary Irish Consul and President of the Irish Institute of Pittsburgh, recognised the potential that existed to create a greater degree of connectivity between Pittsburgh and County Mayo / Ireland West, based on what he termed "this amazing story". Mr Lamb arranged a series

Prof. Andrew Masich, President and C.E.O. of the Heinz History Centre, is presented with a copy of 'The Ultimate Guide to Mayo' by Michael Larkin.
Pic.: courtesy E. Ruby, Heinz History Center.

of meetings and engagements for me throughout the greater Pittsburgh / Allegheny County region. Some of the many influential personnel I was introduced to included members of the boards of Carlow, Duquesne and Pittsburgh Universities, the Controller of Pittsburgh City Council, the Director of Pittsburgh South Side Chamber of Commerce, the Vice Presidents of Pittsburgh Regional Alliance network and Pittsburgh International Airport and former WTAE - TV news anchor, Ms. Wendy Bell. Being invited by the President of the Fort Pitt Pioneer Chapter to speak at their luncheon was extremely special. In the magnificent Senator John Heinz History Center, I was delighted to have met with its President and C.E.O. Prof. Andrew E. Masich, Mr

Mr Jim Lamb, Honorary Consul of Ireland & President of the Irish Institute of Pittsburgh, together with Michael Larkin, photographed in Pittsburgh City Council office. The Coat of Arms of the city of Pittsburgh is visible in the background.
Pic.: courtesy Pittsburgh City Council.

Matthew Strauss, Chief Archivist and Ms. Emily Ruby, Curator. In the Carnegie Library on Forbes Avenue, Ms. Cindy Ulrich, Senior Librarian, handed me transcripts of Thomas Larkin's application for U.S. citizenship and his World War I draft registration form. During the latter years of World War 1, it was mandatory for all able bodied young men throughout the U.S.A. to register and prepare for 'call up' to the American defence forces. Thomas Larkin, along with a regiment of over 2,000 other young men, awaited conscription. However, the welcome news of World War 1 ending on November 11th, 1918, signalled the end of conscription. What a relief it must have been!

Up to this point, all I was aware of was that Thomas Larkin resided in Pittsburgh and was an employee of the Bell Telephone Company of Pennsylvania. Spending time carefully perusing his many old application forms and documents, witnessing his handwriting, his confirmation that Mrs Mary Larkin, County Mayo, Ireland, was his nearest relative, and seeing the date of his arrival in the state of Pennsylvania, May 25th, 1899, was truly very special. Further viewing of those faded and worn documents revealed the addresses and street numbers on Pittsburgh's South Side, where this man had resided during his career with the Bell Telephone Company - again one of those never to be forgotten moments. Later, I was shown a map, and vintage photographs from this region of Pittsburgh in the early 1900s, and contrasting images of today's vibrant and bustling South Side, with its excellently preserved Historical District, along East Carson Street.

Author Michael Larkin underneath the Larkins Way sign
Pic.: courtesy G. McLaughlin, Fort Pitt Pioneers.

However, one street name stood out amongst all others here ... Larkins Way! Thomas Larkin, along with thousands of other immigrant workers, would have walked the cobbled streets of this industrial heartland in Pittsburgh on a daily basis, including the street named 'Larkins Way'.

Chapter 8. *My Journey*

Work Registration Card. *Pic.: courtesy Carnegie Library Pittsburgh.*

Thomas Larkin's mother, Mary. *Pic.: Michael Larkin.*

Residence 141. *Pic.: courtesy Fort Pitt Pioneers.*

Above, Michael Larkin is photographed outside residence number 141 on 19th Street, Pittsburgh. This address appears on Thomas Larkin's work registration card (pictured top left).

Pictured top left, Thomas Larkin's work registration card, naming his mother, Mary Larkin, Mayo, Ireland as his nearest relative. Following his emigration, Mary Larkin (pictured left) would never see her son Thomas again. With all contact having been lost, it was reported that around the fireside following evening prayer, Mary Larkin would say "Thomas, if you're alive somewhere in America, I hope you're doing well. If you're dead, I hope you're in Heaven". Sadly, by the time Thomas had re - established contact, his mother had long since passed away. Note the traditional dress of the time, including the handwoven Irish shawl.

Chapter 8. *My Journey*

Above: Thomas Larkin's U.S. Declaration of Intention form
Pic.: courtesy Carnegie Library Pittsburgh.

Right: Thomas Larkin's Petition of Naturalisation application form to become a Citizen of the United States of America.
Pic.: courtesy Carnegie Library Pittsburgh.

The President of the Fort Pitt Pioneer Chapter, Ms. Gerry McLaughlin accepts a handcrafted Mayo wooden clock from Michael Larkin, on the steps of residence number 97 on 21st Street Pittsburgh. This is the address given by Thomas Larkin on his U.S. Declaration of Intention form (pictured left).
Pic.: courtesy Fort Pitt Pioneers.

Chapter 8. My Journey

Mr Peter Gilmore, Adjunct Prof. of History, Carlow University accepts a piece of Mayo woodcraft from Michael Larkin.
Pic.: courtesy Carlow University.

WALKING IN THE FOOTSTEPS

Pittsburgh's South Side today, with its vibrant, attractive and well planned complex of retail, residential and office developments, is in stark contrast to the South Side of the 1900s. At that time thousands of immigrants were employed in the iron and steel, and other labour intensive industries. Walking along Larkin's Way, standing outside the now very modern apartment where Thomas Larkin once resided, in the company of the President of the Fort Pitt. Pioneer Chapter, was simply an occasion to savour, and made this journey to Pittsburgh so worthwhile.

Strolling slowly along some of the side streets and later along the cultural and cosmopolitan Carson Street, with its beautiful restaurants, fashion and retail outlets, art galleries and boutiques, was both nostalgic and special. Later, over a delightful Americano coffee, in the company of Mr Peter Gilmore, Prof. of History at Carlow University, which was founded in Pittsburgh by the Irish Sisters of Mercy in 1929, Prof. Gilmore outlined that in the early 1900s working shifts from 6am – 6.45pm was commonplace with an average daily wage of $1.50 or $200 - $400 annually, depending on level of skill.

Cobbled streets, smoke stacks, horse carts and street cars, rail tracks and perhaps the occasional Model T. Ford motor car, would have been the main feature in this industrial heartland at the time. Eggs at 34c / doz., milk at 18c per gallon, coffee at 30c per pound, sugar at 8c per pound and many other basic food items were being sold from market stalls in this region [1915 U.S. Census Bureau]. East Carson Street today is a nationally designated Historical District, ensuring that this once thriving industrial region's past will never be forgotten.

My Pittsburgh 'journey of connectivity' was now coming to a close. Wonderful memories, special friends, connectivity with the past re-established and new connections between Pittsburgh and County Mayo created. It was time to say farewell Pittsburgh ... for now!

Achieving that goal of re-connecting with Pittsburgh was extremely special. However, despite the many highs on the journey, it was now time to scale even greater heights!. The next stage on this journey was a 1,400 mile (2,250km), two and a half hour flight westwards, to the Telephone Pioneers of America Headquarters in Denver, Colorado.

Chapter 8. *My Journey*

The city of Denver, with the snow capped Colorado Mountains in the background.
Pic.: Pixabay

Chapter 8. *My Journey*

The Executive Director and members of staff from the Pioneers welcome Michael Larkin to their Headquarters in Denver.
Pic.: courtesy Pioneer Headquarters, Denver.

The Mile High City of Denver

Denver, frequently referred to as the 'mile high city' is situated exactly one mile (5,280ft.) above sea level, making it the highest major city in the U.S.A. The city and its greater metropolitan hinterland has a population of over 2.8 million people.

It grew from a smaller settlement, following the discovery of gold in the region in 1858. Unfortunately, shortly after my arrival in the city, Mr Dan Katze, Vice President of the Pioneers, who I was scheduled to meet, was unavoidably delayed in Florida where he was attending a conference. Despite having arrived in the 'mile high city', I was quickly

Ms. Charlene Hill, Executive Director of the Telephone Pioneers and author Michael Larkin.
Pic.: courtesy Pioneer Headquarters, Denver.

brought 'down to earth' with this revelation. Would my journey to Denver be in vain? Would I be departing Denver without setting foot in the Pioneer Headquarters? However, there was no need to worry. Very soon, I discovered that I would be reaching even further into the clear blue Denver sky! The Headquarters of the Pioneers are located in the 54 storey, 710ft (216m) high, California Street skyscraper - one of the tallest buildings in Denver!

As the giant plate glass doors opened when I arrived at this towering structure of concrete, steel and glass, in its vast foyer I eagerly scanned the directory listing of offices and suites. My entire focus was to locate Suite 225, the Headquarters of the Pioneers, as quickly as possible. Nervously pressing the elevator button at least 4 or 5 times, the doors eventually opened - I was on my way!

Exiting from the elevator and walking swiftly through the winding corridors, there it was in the distance - Suite 225. With an accelerated heart beat and a sense of nervous expectation, I gently knocked on the door of Suite 225. Here I was greeted by Ms. Shirley Zunich, a member of the administrative staff - then I realised my trip to Denver had not been in vain! Ms. Zunich ushered me into their headquarters and introduced me to some of her colleagues.

In another one of those unforgettable moments, meeting Ms Charlene Hill, Executive Director of the Telephone Pioneers, and later being invited into the impressive meeting room to share Thomas Larkin's pioneering journey with officers and staff, was very special. In the background a lifesize painting of telephone pioneer Angus MacDonald entitled 'The Spirit of Service', was truly spectacular. MacDonald was one of the very early telephone linemen, who, along with his crew, went beyond the call of duty to bring food and water to the passengers on board the stalled train on the New York - Boston rail line, during the March 1888 snow blizzard.

This painting, commissioned by AT&T, symbolises the strong work ethic of the early Telephone Pioneers. This iconic image also appears on the certificate presented to Thomas Larkin.

After some photographs and an exchange of gifts, it was time to move along and discover a little more of Denver's many sights and attractions. During my short time in this part of the American Mid West, I was hosted by Richard and Kathleen Mahony and their daughter, Eileen, in their beautiful home in Centennial, South of Denver. Richard and Kathleen have been family acquaintances for years.

The days went by very quickly and it was soon time to say farewell to Denver and continue this journey to Seattle on America's North West Pacific coast.

A long standing invitation to visit some close friends in the State of Washington was not to be overlooked - after all it was only a 1,000 mile (1,600km) westwards journey across the snow capped Rocky Mountains! Seattle, nicknamed the Emerald City, is one of the largest cities on the North West Pacific coast, located only 100 miles (160km) south from the Canada / United States border.

Chapter 8. *My Journey*

Michael Larkin stands alongside Seattle's Monorail. The early Monorail prototypes were designed by Castlebar-native Louis Brennan.
Pic.: courtesy P. Keeshan - Sands.

Plaque commemorating Louis Brennan's birthplace in Castlebar, County Mayo, January 28th, 1852.
Pic.: Michael Larkin

THERE'S ALWAYS A 'NEW CONNECTION'

While the main theme throughout this book is intended to be a 'journey of connectivity' / 'a voyage of discovery' relating to Thomas Larkin's career as a Telephone Pioneer of America, in addition to an outline of significant milestones in the evolution of telecommunications, many other 'connections' also emerge. Westport, 100 miles (160km) west of Seattle, similar to our 'own' Westport in County Mayo, is a very attractive seaport city, with a beautiful bay and marina. It is also the most 'Westerly Westport' in the world!

Visiting Seattle without travelling on the Monorail would be a missed opportunity. Inventor extraordinaire, Louis Brennan (1852 – 1932) was born in Castlebar, County Mayo. A talented innovator, he became known as the 'Monorail Man' for his invention of a 'gyroscopically balanced Monorail', which he patented in 1903. Unfortunately, due to lack of investment and the outbreak of World War I, his invention didn't become a commercial success until many years following his death. The Seattle Monorail was completed in 1962 as an efficient form of transport for the millions of people who attended the Seattle World Exposition that same year. This exposition was similar in magnitude to the giant Philadelphia Centennial Exposition, where Alexander G. Bell demonstrated his 'new invention' to thousands of curious onlookers. Louis Brennan invested a considerable amount of energy and finance into the Monorail project and was eventually forced to sell the family home. He was tragically killed in a motor vehicle accident in 1932. Being almost destitute at the time, he was buried in an unmarked grave in London. In March 2014, he received

Michael Larkin stands at the entrance to the giant Microsoft plant in Seattle. *Pic.: courtesy P. Keeshan - Sands.*

Long time family friend and wonderful host, Mr Patrick Sands, Data and Analytics Engineering Manager, Microsoft, accepts a Mayo.ie information pack from Michael Larkin. *Pic.: courtesy Patricia Keeshan Sands.*

the acknowledgement he so rightly deserved, when a new headstone on his grave was unveiled by An Taoiseach, Mr Enda Kenny. A plaque was also unveiled at his birthplace in Castlebar. Meanwhile, Seattle's Monorail continues to roll along over 5th Avenue, overlooking this beautiful city!

Many of the world's most recognisable names in technology including Amazon, Facebook, Google and Microsoft have a significant presence in this region. The evolution of the telephone industry from the days of Alexander G. Bell and the phenomenal growth of the computer industry more recently are strikingly similar.

Mr Patrick Sands, Engineering Manager in Data and Analytics at Microsoft, provided me with an awe-inspiring tour, and outlined the history of Microsoft since its foundation in 1975 by Seattle friends Paul Allen and Bill Gates. In many respects Mr Gates and Mr Allen as co-founders of Microsoft, were the equivalent of A.G. Bell and Thomas Watson. Patrick Sands and his fellow employees are today's equivalent of the Telephone Pioneers of the past. In a similar way to the evolution of the telephone from the time of its invention, the following predictions reflect opinion at a time when computer development was in its infancy

"There is no need for any individual to have a computer in his home" (Ken Olsen, Founder and President, Digital Corp.),

"Computers in the future may weigh as little as 1.5 tons" (Popular Mechanics magazine forecasting the rapid use of technology 1949)

"I think there may be a world market for maybe five computers" (Thomas Watson Chairman IBM 1943).

Chapter 8. *My Journey*

Giant Machines in the Sky

When Alexander G. Bell predicted that "In the not too distant future I believe it will be possible to have dinner in New York at 7 o'clock in the evening and breakfast in Dublin or London the following morning", few, including Mr Bell, could envisage that 'giant machines' in the sky, as large as ocean liners, would circumnavigate the earth. The largest building by volume in the world, the Boeing Aircraft Manufacturing Plant, is located in Everett, 25 miles (40km) north of Seattle. The complex, covering an area of 100 acres (40.5ha.) employs over 30,000 people and commenced operations in 1943. On a guided tour of this giant manufacturing complex, it was most interesting to note a significant Irish connection. Ryanair, Ireland's low cost airline, is one of Boeing's largest customers, having signed a $20 billion contract in 2014 for the delivery of 175 new Boeing 737 jet airplanes.

Across the Atlantic Ocean, in Thomas Larkin's native County of Mayo, high on what was once termed 'a foggy, boggy hill', Ireland West Airport Knock (I.W.A.K.), now stands. This international airport, when first mooted by Fr. James Horan, (later to be known as Monsignor Horan), who was born in the village of Partry, only 4 miles (6.5km) from the Larkin homestead, was deemed to be both unrealistic and unworkable. Today, many of the Boeing aircraft assembled in the giant manufacturing plant near Seattle arrive and depart on a daily basis from this airport. The book 'On a Wing and a Prayer' by Terry Reilly tells Monsignor Horan's life story and the building of this airport. 'On a Wing and a Prayer - The Musical', based on this book, was adapted for stage by its author, in collaboration with award-winning broadcaster Tommy Marren. It celebrates in song and story the building of this 'Miracle' airport. The world premiere of the musical was held in Castlebar, in November 2010. Today, the Emerald City of Seattle is connected to the Emerald Isle of Ireland via direct, non-stop transatlantic flights. In 2017, former U.S. Vice President Joe Biden touched down at Ireland West Airport Knock, as he made a nostalgic journey 'home', to connect with his Mayo roots. The airport also welcomed Pope Francis on the occasion of his visit to Knock Shrine in August 2018. Knock Shrine is visited by over 1,000,000 people annually, its Basilica being the largest ecclesiastical structure in Ireland.

Pictured in the Boeing headquarters in Everett.
Pic.: courtesy P. Keeshan - Sands

Irish Organisations and Associations in Seattle

Seattle has a large number of vibrant and active Irish networks and associations. This fact was acknowledged during official visits to the city by An Taoiseach, Mr Enda Kenny in 2014 and President Michael D. Higgins in 2015. The Honorary Irish Consul in Seattle, Mr John F. Keane, speaking at a luncheon, also outlined the significant role of many Irish emigrants in Seattle's political and cultural history. Judge Thomas Burke (1849 – 1925), acknowledged as 'the man who built Seattle' dominated economic, social and political life in Seattle in the early 1900s. The Burke museum is named in his honour. John Harte McGraw (1850 - 1910) was the second Governor of Washington State and John Collins (1835 - 1903) was Seattle's 4th Mayor. Today, the Seattle Gaels, Irish Network Seattle and the Irish Heritage Club are some of the networks and associations that continue to promote a positive image of Ireland.

Distant relations and wonderful friends, Mrs Patricia Keeshan-Sands and her family were wonderful hosts for the duration of my time in this region.

Leaving Seattle behind - eastwards bound

It was now time to prepare for the 2,400 mile (3.900km), five hour transcontinental journey eastwards to New York where on November 30th, 1930 Thomas Larkin was conferred with Life Membership of the Telephone Pioneers of America at a ceremony in the American Telegraph and Telephone (AT&T) Headquarters, 195 Broadway Manhattan. The magnificent 29 storey 429ft (198m) high building constructed in 1912, is no longer in the ownership of AT&T. However, its marble clad interior and intricate plasterwork retain the elegance and grandeur of its illustrious past.

At the time of Thomas Larkin's conferring ceremony, a giant bronze sculpture, named the 'Spirit of Communication', second only in size to the Statue of Liberty, sat on the roof of the building. Today, this giant sculpture, covered in gold leaf, stands in the lobby of the AT&T headquarters in Dallas, Texas.

The telephone building, as the skyscraper on 195 Broadway is still known, was the site of many significant milestones in the evolution of telecommunications. On January 25th, 1915 the first transcontinental telephone call was made when Alexander G. Bell called his assistant, Thomas Watson in San Francisco, 3,000 miles (4,900km) to the west. U.S. President Woodrow Wilson, Mayor of New York John Purray Mitchel and members of AT&T management team were present in this building at the time of this first coast-to-coast telephone call. On January 7th, 1927 the first transatlantic telephone call from New York to London was also made from this historic building.

A.I.H.S. The American Irish Historical Society

"I am proud of my membership of this society and I am also proud of the strain of Irish blood in my veins"
(U.S. President Theodre Roosevelt - January 1909).

These words convey President Roosvelt's sense of pride in his Irish roots and his membership of the American Irish

Historical Society (A.I.H.S.) The A.I.H.S. founded in 1897, on New York's 5th Avenue, contains one of the largest collections of Irish historical material in the U.S.A. I had the privilege of meeting with Ms Georgette Keane, Library and Archives Curator, who acknowledged Thomas Larkin's distinguished career as a Telephone Pioneer of America, adding his name to the vast library collection of the A.I.H.S.

I.A.C.I. The Irish American Cultural Institute

The Ireland - U.S. Council, the County Mayo Association of New York, and the Irish-American Heritage Museum, incorporating the Paul O'Dwyer Library, were other eminent organisations and institutions that I was in communication with regarding Thomas Larkin's pioneering journey. The Irish American Cultural Institute (I.A.C.I.) according to their mission statement 'Promote an intelligent appreciation of Ireland, and the role and contribution of the Irish in American Culture'.

The institute, headquartered in New Jersey, with Chapters spread throughout the U.S.A., profiled Thomas Larkin's journey in one of its journals. However, before departure from New York there was still one other site to visit, which has a significant and direct connection to Ireland ... and especially with Thomas Larkin's native County of Mayo!

Michael Larkin stands at the impressive entrance to the American Irish Historical Society, holding a copy of the book 'Ballyheane Past & Present' which he presented to Ms. Georgette Keane, AIHS Curator.
Pic.: Courtesy AIHS Library.

Mastic Shirley to Killala Mayo

"We are like islands in the sea, separate on the surface, connected in the deep" (William James 1842 – 1910).

While the island of Ireland and the 'island' (continent) of North America are indeed 'separate on the surface' of the Atlantic Ocean, we are 'connected in the deep' in a very special way. At Mastic Bay, on Long Island's southern shoreline, the small hamlet of Shirley is uniquely connected with Killala, County Mayo. It is from here that the fiber optic cable stretches 3,400 miles (5,400km) 'in the deep' of the Atlantic ocean to Killala, County Mayo.

"This new cable allows Ireland and her 'exiled children in America' to be even more connected than ever before" (Irish America Magazine - February 2016).

Less than 100 years ago, if the most eagerly awaited handwritten 'letter from America' arrived at its destination in Ireland inside seven days it was considered 'rapid connectivity'. Following the first transatlantic telephone call in 1927 to be connected within seven minutes was regarded as 'rapid connectivity'. Today, the fiber optic cable stretching across the Atlantic Ocean from the eastern shoreline of the U.S.A. to County Mayo's northern coastline, delivers rapid connectivity almost at the speed of light.

Leaving behind this quaint hamlet of Shirley and heading for the bustling and dazzling heart of New York city, I silently pondered - 'What's next in terms of 'rapid connectivity'?

The sign denoting the quiet hamlet of Shirley, on the shores of Mastic Bay, is uniquely connected with Killala, County Mayo, via the transatlantic fiber optic cable.
Pic.: courtesy Gwen R. Pressley.

Chapter 8. *My Journey*

Honorary Membership

New Vision | pioneers
a volunteer network

May it be known that

Michael Larkin

Is hereby proclaimed an Honorary Member of

The Fort Pitt Chapter of

The Telecom Pioneers of America

And is thus accorded the fellowship and

privileges of such membership

Dated this 7th day of March, 2018

Gerry McLaughlin
President, Fort Pitt Chapter #13, Pittsburgh, Pennsylvania

Being awarded Honorary Membership of the Fort Pitt Chapter of The Telecom Pioneers of America is indeed a special privilege. More than words can describe, this award in many ways made 'my journey' so worthwhile and strengthens even further this very special connection.

9

THOMAS LARKIN'S LEGACY - A SYMBOL OF TRANSATLANTIC CONNECTIVITY

When Thomas Larkin secured employment as a telephone lineman little did he realise that in time his emigrant journey and subsequent career with the Bell Telephone Company of Pennsylvania, would one day be portrayed as a fitting symbol of transatlantic connectivity in its many facets between Ireland and North America.

The American Conference for Irish Studies (A.C.I.S.) is one of the foremost scholarly organisations devoted to the study of Irish American history and migration.

Following my initial correspondence and discussions with members of this esteemed organisation, leading figures from within the A.C.I.S. recognised the symbolism of Thomas Larkin's journey as a vivid illustration of Irish history and migration throughout the centuries.

In June 2018, two leading academics in the field of Irish studies made a very significant and special visit to Mayo, to acknowledge the legacy of this Telephone Pioneer of America.

Professors Timothy McMahon, (left) and Matthew O'Brien are presented with copies of the book 'A Guide to Mayo', by Michael Larkin, on the occasion of their special visit to the county.
Pic.: Michael Donnelly.

Dr. Timothy McMahon, President of the American Conference for Irish Studies and Professor of History at Marquette University, together with Dr. Matthew O'Brien, Pittsburgh, Professor of History at Steubenville University, were accorded a Civic Welcome by members of Castlebar Municipal District Council following their arrival in Castlebar.

Chapter 9. *Thomas Larkin's Legacy*

Both academics also visited a number of County Mayo's iconic, historical landmarks, including the Foxford Woollen Mills, Michael Davitt Museum in Straide, the Martin Sheridan sculpture, Bohola, Ballintubber Abbey, and enjoyed a walk around the tranquil waters of Lough Lannagh.

In the Galway Mayo Institute of Technology (G.M.I.T.), both Professors delivered a series of lectures and provided a fascinating insight into Irish migration patterns, transatlantic connectivity between Ireland and North America, and the legacy of Thomas Larkin as a Telephone Pioneer of America.

However, the true symbolism of this man's journey to the

Mr Michael Gill, Acting Head of the Galway Mayo Institute of Technology (G.M.I.T.), welcomes Professors Timothy McMahon and Matthew O'Brien to the Mayo Campus.
Pic.: Michael Donnelly.

Castlebar Municipal District Council accords a Civic Welcome to Professors McMahon and O'Brien in Lough Lannagh Village.
Front, left to right; Ms. Helena McArdle, Prof. Matthew O'Brien, Cllr. Martin McLoughlin, Cathaoirleach of Castlebar Municipal District Council, Prof. Timothy McMahon, Michael Larkin and Ms. Alice Rowley, Chairperson of Killawalla Community Council.
Back, left to right; Pat Staunton, Ms. Caitriona Doyle, Cllr. Al McDonnell, John McHale, Acting Head of Castlebar Municipal District, Deputy Lisa Chambers T.D., Opposition Spokesperson on Brexit, Cllrs. Frank Durcan, Michael Kilcoyne, Blackie Gavin, Henry Kenny, Joe McHale, Neil Sheridan, Communications and Diaspora Officer, Mayo County Council, and Micheál Larkin.
Pic.: Michael Donnelly.

U.S.A. was recognised, when both academics visited the ancestral homestead of Thomas Larkin, 'walked' in many of the footsteps and 'stood' on the ground, once so familiar to Thomas Larkin.

This significant visit, coupled with the visit by the President of the Fort Pitt Telephone Pioneer Chapter, Ms. Gerry McLaughlin in 2016, fosters and preserves this 'special connection' as a symbol of Irish connectedness, throughout the world. Their visit culminated with a silent reflection at the headstone of Thomas Larkin in Killawalla cemetery.

Where the story began! Pictured at the entrance to the old Larkin homestead in Derrew, *left to right* Shane Larkin, Matthew O'Brien, Michael Larkin, Timothy McMahon and Micheál Larkin.
Pic.: Michael Donnelly.

Some of the attendees at the lectures delivered by Professors McMahon and O'Brien. *Front, left to right;* Prof. Timothy McMahon, Michael Gill, Acting Head of the G.M.I.T., and Prof. Matthew O'Brien. *Second row;* Terry Reilly, former editor Western People newspaper, Michael and Micheál Larkin. *Third row;* John Callaghan, Anne O'Malley, Seán Ó Conaghaile and Caitriona Doyle. *Fourth row;* Ronan O'Malley, Pat Staunton and Shane Larkin.
Pic.: Michael Donnelly.

Professors O'Brien and McMahon hold the impressive Pennsylvania Cup, which was presented to the captain of the Mayo Senior Football team on the occasion of their visit to the U.S.A. in 1932.
Pic.: Michael Donnelly.

Chapter 9. *Thomas Larkin's Legacy*

Hereford cattle enjoy a 'treat' from Prof. Matthew O'Brien on the Larkin family farm.
Pic.: Michael Donnelly.

A UNIQUE TAPESTRY OF CONNECTIVITY

The degree of connectivity between Ireland and its diaspora throughout the world is extremely strong. As a consequence of our long history of emigration and having much in common in terms of language, identity and culture, that bond of connectivity is especially strong with Great Britain and North America. The appointment of a Minister with specific responsibility for our diaspora demonstrates the commitment of the Irish Government in fostering and preserving connectivity with our emigrants throughout the world.

'Mayo - the Connected County' was the theme of the 2014 World Convention of Mayo Associations, where special guest, His Excellency, Mr Kevin Vickers, Canadian Ambassador to Ireland, outlined the strong bonds of connectivity that exist between Canada and the island of Ireland.

Signifying the strength of Mayo's connectivity with its diaspora, Mayo World Conventions have been held in many parts of the world, including Toronto, Manchester,

His Excellency Mr Kevin Vickers, Canadian Ambassador to Ireland, together with Michael Larkin, hold a framed photograph of Thomas Larkin. Pic.: John Moylette.

Philadelphia, Buenos Aires, Cleveland and County Mayo. Also of major significance in terms of connectivity is the hugely successful 'Mayo Day' initiative, spearheaded by Mayo County Council, which is a global celebration of 'Mayoness' amongst our diaspora throughout the world.

Chapter 10. *Tapestry of Connectivity*

The $300 million Transatlantic fiber optic cable project places County Mayo at the epicentre of a unique connection linking Europe and the U.S.A. When the cable reached landfall in Killala, County Mayo, Mr Greg Varisco, Chief Operations Officer of Aqua Comms stated;

"this is a project that will cover the needs of tomorrow, today".

In what is an amazing tapestry of connectivity uniquely linking County Mayo and the U.S.A., Thomas Larkin delivered what was at the time 'the most modern form of connectivity in the world into the American Mid West.

Today, his native County of Mayo is central to the delivery of what is now 'the most modern form of connectivity in the world' between Europe and the U.S.A.

"BELIEVE ME, THE DAY WILL COME WHEN YOU WILL BE ABLE TO 'SEE' THE PERSON WHO YOU ARE SPEAKING TO ON THE TELEPHONE".

When Thomas Larkin uttered the above words, following his retirement and return to a predominantly rural Ireland, they were greeted with suspicion and laughter.

Perhaps if he could now 'see' the advances in telecommunications and the arrival of the new transatlantic fiber optic cable to his native County Mayo he might smile and say, "I told you so".

Majestic cliffs west of Downpatrick Head 'welcome' the arrival of the transatlantic fiber optic cable. To you, the reader of this book, a similar warm and special welcome awaits for you to discover and explore County Mayo, the heartbeat of Ireland's Wild Atlantic Way.
Pic.: Michael Larkin.

11

REFLECTION

"Some say 'never look back'-
but when we do, it's so satisfying to realise how far we've come".

Richelle E. Goodrich

As we approach the end of this book, perhaps it's a good time to reflect on the term 'connectivity' in its broadest sense and the importance of making the 'right connections' in our everyday lifestyles, career, relationships, etc.

During his time as a telephone lineman with the Bell Telephone Company, Thomas Larkin made thousands of cable connections which enabled the sound of a human voice to be heard over a wire, in a matter of minutes. However, despite making many connections, for a time he lost that most important connection of all ... the connection with his homeland and family.

Nowadays, many different forms of technology allow us to establish worldwide connectivity in microseconds.

Yes, today's rapidly changing world of modern technology means that we are more connected than ever ... or are we? Are we becoming increasingly reliant on social media, rather than face-to-face interaction? That deep human connection, much deeper than any transatlantic cable, made by the sound of our voice over the telephone, listening to, or spending time with real friends, will always be the most fundamental form of connectivity. Remaining connected with family and friends, becoming involved in activities within our neighbourhood, connectivity with our diaspora, befriending an elderly person or neighbour in our community ... this is real connectivity which has stood the test of time.

Embracing today's rapidly evolving forms of technology is important ... more important still, is never forgetting the simplicity of the spoken word. It's all about 'Making the Right Connections'.

"Often we look so long and so regretfully upon the closed door, that we fail to see the doors which open for us".
(Alexander G. Bell)

AN ODE TO THE TELEPHONE PIONEERS OF YESTERYEAR

By Michael Larkin

Those telephone poles have had their day,

I hear you say.

Leaning now towards earth,

That once gave them their birth,

As Douglas fir or Lodgepole pine,

They reached into the skyline,

Carrying their wires of copper,

They once stood tall and proper.

Now overgrown by woodland green,

As one walks along the narrow boreen.

Hush! You can almost hear the harsh grating sound,

Of the shovel and spade, as they dug this stoney ground.

The telephone man, Alexander Graham Bell,

He was told 'there isn't a chance in hell',

That this telephone device,

Will ever carry the sound of a human voice.